THE WORLD OF WAL-MART

"Incisive, vividly analyzed, and utterly teachable, this book examines Wal-Mart as a product and producer of contemporary American society. Probing how Wal-Mart works from production to consumption to public relations, this outstanding book offers far-reaching arguments about the power and influence of corporations and the politics of freedom, labor, and value in the United States today."

—Peter Benson, Anthropology, *Washington University in Saint Louis*

"Told with verve and momentum, this gem of a book is ideal for the classroom. It does an exceptional job of showing how America made Wal-Mart, and how Wal-Mart made America. Along the way, *The World of Wal-Mart* demonstrates why anthropology in particular is well-suited for making sense of the world we live in."

—Steve Striffler, Latin American Studies, *University of New Orleans*

This book demonstrates the usefulness of anthropological concepts by taking a critical look at Wal-Mart and the American Dream. Rather than singling Wal-Mart out for criticism, the authors treat the company as a product of a socio-political order that it also helps to shape. The book attributes Wal-Mart's success to the failure of American (and global) society to make the Dream available to everyone. It shows how decades of neoliberal economic policies have exposed contradictions at the heart of the Dream, creating an opening for Wal-Mart. The company's success has generated a host of negative externalities, however, fueling popular ambivalence and organized opposition.

The World of Wal-Mart also describes the strategies that Wal-Mart uses to maintain legitimacy, fend off unions, enter new markets, and cultivate an aura of benevolence and ordinariness, despite these externalities. It focuses on Wal-Mart's efforts to forge symbolic and affective inclusion, and on their self-promotion as a free market solution to the social problems of poverty, inequality, and environmental destruction. Finally, the book contrasts the conceptions of freedom and human rights that underlie Wal-Mart's business model with the alternative visions of freedom forwarded by their critics.

Nicholas Copeland is a social anthropologist at Virginia Polytechnic University. His research about state power and Maya politics in Guatemala appears in the *Journal of Latin American Studies* and *Development and Change*. Nick taught at the University of Arkansas, and has conducted extensive market research inside Wal-Mart.

Christine Labuski is an anthropologist and Assistant Professor in Women's and Gender Studies at Virginia Polytechnic University. Her work can be found in *Feminist Studies, Archives of Sexual Behavior*, and several edited volumes about the gendered body. She has also spent countless hours inside Wal-Mart stores as a market researcher.

The Routledge Series for Creative Teaching and Learning in Anthropology

Editor: Richard H. Robbins, SUNY Plattsburgh

This series is dedicated to innovative, unconventional ways to connect undergraduate students and their lived concerns about our social world to the power of social science ideas and evidence. Our goal is to help spark social science imaginations and, in doing so, open new avenues for meaningful thought and action.

First published 2013
by Routledge
711 Third Avenue, New York, NY 10017

Simultaneously published in the UK
by Routledge
2 Park Square, Milton Park, Abingdon, Oxon OX14 4RN

Routledge is an imprint of the Taylor & Francis Group, an informa business

© 2013 Taylor & Francis

Library of Congress Cataloging in Publication Data
Copeland, Nicholas.
  The world of Wal-Mart/Nicholas Copeland and Christine Labuski.
  p. cm.—(Routledge series for creative teaching and learning in
  anthropology)
  Includes bibliographical references and index.
  1. Wal-Mart (Firm)—History. 2. Discount houses (Retail trade)—
  United States. 3. Business anthropology—United States.
  4. Corporate culture—United States. 5. Consumption
  (Economics)—United States. 6. United States—Social life and
  customs. I. Labuski, Christine. II. Title.
  HF5429.215.U6C68 2013
  381′.1490973—dc23
  2012028229

ISBN: 978-0-415-89487-6 (hbk)
ISBN: 978-0-415-89488-3 (pbk)
ISBN: 978-0-203-07218-9 (ebk)

Typeset in New Baskerville
by Florence Production Ltd, Stoodleigh, Devon, UK

THE WORLD OF WAL-MART

Discounting the American Dream

*Nicholas Copeland and
Christine Labuski*

Routledge
Taylor & Francis Group

NEW YORK AND LONDON

CONTENTS

ACKNOWLEDGMENTS

We are indebted to a number of individuals who helped to make this book a reality. First among these is Jodi O'Brien, who took an idea that she heard over drinks seriously enough to pass it along to someone who had the capacity to make it happen. We are also grateful to our editor Steve Rutter and to the series editor Richard Robbins for their commitment to the project and for their stewardship, especially for their suggestions about how to make the manuscript as accessible as possible. We are also grateful to Samantha Barbaro at Routledge for all of her assistance.

We could not have written this book without Kathleen Stewart, whose remarkable ability to appreciate the miraculous in the ordinary, provided us with an indispensable lens for thinking about Wal-Mart. We are also thankful to Katie, Ronn, and Ariana for generously allowing us to write much of this book in their welcoming home during two scorching Austin summers. And we want to thank all of our Austin friends who provided ideas, support, and necessary distractions while we wrote, especially: Melissa Biggs, Beth Bruinsma Chang, Chris Carty, Jim Coupal, Jacob Childress, Tamara Goheen, Celeste Henery, Alia Hasan Khan, Kathleen McCarthy, Chris McNett, Anne Merrill, Alisa Perkins, Vivian Newdick, Billy O'Leary, Mubbashir Rizvi, Karla Steffen, Nathan Tabor, John Toole, Teresa Velasquez, and Jackie Zahn. Special thanks go to Pablo Gonzales for alerting us to Wal-Mart's connection to events in Atenco, Mexico, and to Diya Mehra for her suggestion that we investigate Wal-Mart's attempts to break into the Indian retail market.

Writing a book about Wal-Mart as visiting faculty at the University of Arkansas often made us feel like spies with a dangerous yet delicious mission. We are grateful to scores of friends and co-conspirators at the "You of A" and in Fayetteville, many of whom helped with photos, scouting trips Bentonville, and other logistical support. These include: Ted Swedenburg, Rob Brubaker, Troy Gittings, Marta Kiser, and Misty Hale Gittings. We also want to thank the many, many folks who listened patiently while we talked through the ideas in this book, and who shared their own cultural knowledge of Wal-Mart and northwest Arkansas, including: Kirstin Erickson, Lisa Corrigan, Kelly O'Callaghan, Mike Pierce, Laurent Sacharoff, Janine Parry, Bill Schreckhise, Andy Horowitz, Salar Jahedi, Stuart Fulbright, Jesse Casana, Sabrina Billings, Alex Pappas, Jeff Gringas, Kendall Curlee, and Chaim Goodman-Strauss. We were especially fortunate to have Raja Swamy as our interlocutor, colleague, and comrade during these years, and we are grateful for his important insights regarding the politics of India's Public Distribution System.

Brittany Phillips and Erin Von Feldt made life in Fayetteville especially meaningful and memorable. We are so grateful to them for sharing their home and their lives with us and we miss them dearly. We also extend a heartfelt thanks to the NWA Workers' Justice Center, and to Fernando Morales in particular, for fighting for workers' rights in the shadow of Wal-Mart, and for first introducing us to OUR Wal-Mart. Lisa Sharp and Nightbird Books deserve an extra dose of gratitude for providing an ideal public space for these folks to tell an alternative story at the 2012 Annual Shareholders Meeting.

And finally, we want to thank our families for their constant support; their respective relationships with Wal-Mart have shaped this story in many ways.

SERIES FOREWORD

The premise of these short books on the anthropology of stuff is that stuff talks, that written into the biographies of everyday items of our lives—coffee, T-shirts, computers, iPods, flowers, drugs, coffee, and so forth—are the stories that make us who we are and that make the world the way it is. From their beginnings, each item bears the signature of the people who extracted, manufactured, picked, caught, assembled, packaged, delivered, purchased and disposed of it. And in our modern market-driven societies, our lives are dominated by the pursuit of stuff.

Examining stuff is also an excellent way to teach and learn about what is exciting and insightful about anthropological and sociological ways of knowing. Students, as with virtually all of us, can relate to stuff, while, at the same time, discovering through these books that it can provide new and fascinating ways of looking at the world.

Stuff, or commodities and things are central, of course, to all societies, to one extent or another. Whether it is yams, necklaces, horses, cattle, or shells, the acquisition, accumulation and exchange of things is central to the identities and relationships that tie people together and drive their behavior. But never, before now, has the craving for stuff reached the level it has; and never before have so many people been trying to convince each other that acquiring more stuff is what they most want to do. As a consequence, the creation, consumption and disposal of stuff now threatens the planet itself. Yet to stop or even slow down the manufacture, sale and accumulation of stuff would threaten the viability of our economy, on which our society is built.

This raises various questions. For example, what impact does the compulsion to acquire stuff have on our economic, social and political well-being, as well as on our environment? How do we come to believe that there are certain things that we must have? How do we come to value some commodities or form of commodities above others? How have we managed to create commodity chains that link peasant farmers in Colombia or gold miners in Angola to wealthy residents of New York, brides in India or teenagers in Nebraska? Who comes up with the ideas for stuff and how do they translate those ideas into things for people to buy? Why do we sometimes consume stuff that is not very good for us? These short books examine such questions, and more.

In this book about Wal-Mart, Nick Copeland and Christine Labuski provide a glimpse inside an organization central to a culture in which access to stuff comprises a major element of the good life, or, in their terms, the "American dream." Wal-Mart provides stuff cheap. Or, as former U.S. labor secretary Robert B. Reich said, "Wal-Mart is the logical end point and the future of the economy in a society whose preeminent value is getting the best deal."

The problem, as Copeland and Labuski demonstrate, is that fulfilling the American Dream with low prices, sometimes means making life miserable for others. For Americans, this poses problems: how can we reconcile our values of freedom, prosperity and inclusion with the kind of consumerism made possible by companies such as Wal-Mart? How do we reconcile our faith in free markets with the idea that people should labor under dignified conditions? And how do we reconcile our desire to support local labor, when the stuff we buy is manufactured on the other side of the globe by largely non-unionized workers?

Wal-Mart, Copeland and Labuski suggest, is the ideal place to examine these contradictions and the discomfort they sometimes produce. Wal-Mart is not only huge (the third largest company in the world with over 2 million employees), but it has forged an intimate association with brand "America," linking success with American economic and religious beliefs and values. Yet, as the authors demonstrate, Wal-Mart relies on millions of low-income workers, as well as customers sometimes dependent on Wal-Mart's low prices to make ends meet.

The World of Wal-Mart: Discounting the American Dream is a perfect complement to anthropology and sociology courses that help students critically examine their own lives and cultures and to understand the connections between their lives and those of others around the world.

Richard H. Robbins,
State University of New York,
Plattsburgh

PREFACE

"You're writing a book about what?" Given that both of us spend the majority of our professional time researching other topics (gender and sexuality for Labuski; indigenous politics, state power, and populism in Guatemala for Copeland), we have grown accustomed to hearing this question from friends and colleagues. One simple response is that Wal-Mart touches on matters that are of great interest to both of us. For example, not only was Wal-Mart recently embroiled in the largest gender discrimination lawsuit in history, they also practice some of the most successful forms of rural populism in the contemporary United States.

More broadly, Wal-Mart's success raises scores of important questions about inequality, collective action, globalization, power, space, and freedom that relate not only to our own research, but also to the major political questions of our time. Not surprisingly, these are also the core issues covered in introductory anthropology and sociology classes. Unpacking the size, success, and ordinariness of a taken for granted institution like Wal-Mart provides an ideal opportunity to concretely address these topics in ways that spark the social scientific imagination—showing students how Wal-Mart is shaped by American society, as well as by a particular conception of the American Dream, while is at the same time reconfiguring both. Because so many students work at, shop in, or at least live near one of the company's four thousand plus stores, Wal-Mart helps bring anthropological and sociological concepts to life in ways that matter and make sense in their everyday lives. In addition, rather than treating Wal-Mart as inevitable, the book introduces students to alternative and often overlooked ways of organizing social, economic, and political life that exist in tension with Wal-Mart's high volume, high efficiency business model.

As authors, we had different histories with Wal-Mart: Christine did not grow up shopping there and found it easy to boycott the company because of their labor rights record and supply chain abuses. Nick, on the other hand, grew up in Lewisville, Texas, a class conscious Dallas suburb where Wal-Mart anchored the strip mall-lined main street, and where kids made fun of other kids' parents for shopping there. He lived around the corner from a Wal-Mart in high school, and his brother Scott worked at a supercenter for several years. Talk about shopping, working, stealing, quitting, or getting fired from Wal-Mart, in addition to frequent soliloquies about the store's impact on the town and on residents' lives (both good and bad), was part of the daily routine.

Our curiosity about the forces that make Wal-Mart possible, and what it was doing to society, occurred to us many times when, as graduate students at the University of Texas, we worked part-time as market researchers. This work often took place inside Wal-Mart stores and involved close and extended contact with the residents of Wal-Mart country—we talked with shoppers about their habits and desires and closely observed them as they navigated aisles full of eye catching products. Watching thousands of customers parade through the stores' sliding glass doors on hot summer days, we contemplated the meaning and magic of Wal-Mart, and of consumer capitalism itself.

But we probably would not have written a book had we not lived in Northwest Arkansas, the epicenter of Wal-Mart country. Not only did we have ready access to Wal-Mart's hometown of Bentonville, we also saw its effects on the landscape and heard scores of debates about the retailer, from partisans and detractors as well as vendors and executives. We also watched as our town was utterly transformed over the course of two Annual Shareholders Meetings. At the University of Arkansas, where we worked, the business school is named after "Mr. Sam," basketball games are played in the Bud Walton Arena, and the Wal-Mart Foundation donated hundreds of millions of dollars to the school's endowment. We attended concerts at the Walton Arts Center in Fayetteville, and we witnessed the arrival of the Crystal Bridges Museum of American Art in late 2011. In short, living in Fayetteville allowed us to more deeply—and more locally—appreciate the pervasiveness of Wal-Mart culture.

Finally, this book was significantly shaped by our encounters with the courageous members of OUR Wal-Mart, who we met through our connections with the Northwest Arkansas Workers' Justice Center. We feel very lucky to have been in Fayetteville while this group emerged, and we want to thank them for reminding us that ordinary people can make extraordinary changes at Wal-Mart, even when they seem like an unstoppable force. We dedicate this book to them.

1

WAL-MART'S CULTURAL
POLITICS

Picture yourself at the checkout counter of a Wal-Mart supercenter. For many of us, this task is very easy, given Wal-Mart's place in our everyday lives and routines. The millions who shop at Wal-Mart think of it as the place that has everything: where we go to get what we need and to save money doing it, the familiar giant of the urban landscape. But now imagine that instead of relying on your auto-pilot, "shields up" mode to quickly shuttle you through this experience, you begin to question the ordinariness of your surroundings. You start to wonder how Wal-Mart became so successful, and how the company came to be seen as so unquestionably patriotic. You reflect on the sheer immensity of the store; you think about what used to be in this spot and whether this particular store will even be here ten years from now. You ponder the deliberate crafting of the thousands of images and sounds that surround you: the bright lights and eye-catching signs, the abundant displays of colorful merchandise, and the advertisements you can hear over the store's loudspeaker—all vying for your attention. You remember feeling genuine warmth on your way into the store as you were greeted by a smiling elderly woman in a blue vest. You also recall the bouts of pleasure, satisfaction, and boredom you experienced as you cruised through the aisles.

In your newly aware state, you take a second look at the laser scanning the UPC codes on your merchandise, and you wonder where that data goes and what happens to it. You ask yourself where the astounding array of products comes from and how they can all be so unbelievably cheap. You also wonder why there are so many security cameras on the walls and who is watching. Listening more carefully, you now notice country music playing softly in the background—audible among the rhythmic checkout beeps. You see a group collecting signatures for a petition at a table outside. You smell the McDonald's™ near the door and wonder about when and how they merged so seamlessly with Wal-Mart. You think about the thousands of people, like yourself, who cycle through this store every day, and about how the entire global economy runs on individual transactions like yours.

Your mind may wander to the negative press that Wal-Mart has drawn over the years: low wages, sweatshops, a Supreme Court case about gender discrimination within the company (the largest class action lawsuit in history), rampant environmental destruction, boarded-up downtowns, and big box sprawl. You recall a popular website that ridicules "people of Wal-Mart" for being low-class and trashy; you wonder if you should join in the derision, or, worse, if these people might be making fun of you. As you reflect, you think about shopping addictions, and you recall reading a news report of a "Black Friday" stampede at a Long Island Wal-Mart, where, in 2008, Haitian immigrant and temporary security guard Jdimytai Damour was trampled to death at 5:00 a.m. by shoppers eager to take advantage of advertised discounts. You remember asking yourself what on earth would compel people to walk right over this wounded man without stopping. Or you know all too well.

You may have read with outrage or with a cynical smirk the news that Wal-Mart was caught bribing Mexican officials, and you remember hearing that Wal-Mart is the largest seller of firearms in the U.S. You might love "your" Wal-Mart, or hate all Wal-Mart's, but it is more likely that you feel a little bit of both. You are inescapably aware of Wal-Mart's enormous size, power, and ubiquity, and are probably curious about what Wal-Mart is doing to us, and to the world we live in. You may find yourself wondering how something so powerful, so multifaceted, so complicated, and even so perverse ever came into being, and then how it came to be so ordinary.

America's Ordinary Behemoth

Wal-Mart is widely known for its folksy atmosphere, patriotism, and Christian family values, and it is famous for prices that are slashed-to-the-bone. The company is an all-pervasive feature of the American landscape and is a juggernaut in the global economy. Wal-Mart is not just big, it is gargantuan, and it has grown impressively since its relatively humble beginnings in Rogers, Arkansas in 1962. In 2010, nearly 100 million customers around the globe shopped at Wal-Mart in an average week, spending approximately $400 billion each year. With $14.3 billion in annual net income and 2.1 million employees, Wal-Mart is the world's largest retailer and grocer, and America's largest private employer. In 2011, Wal-Mart had 696 Discount Stores, 2,928 Supercenters, 609 Sam's Clubs, and 185 Neighborhood Markets in the United States. Wal-Mart is larger than its five biggest competitors *combined*. Wal-Mart owns 9,200 stores in 27 countries (including the U.S.) [www.walmartstores.com/pressroom/FactSheets/] under dozens of names, and its profits far exceed the Gross National Product of many of the countries where it conducts business.

Wal-Mart's immense size makes the company unbelievably powerful. Their sales numbers, buying decisions, and standards reverberate throughout a globally linked supply chain, setting the pace of the retail sector. Their buying power is so immense that one shift can raise or lower commodity prices, and they regularly dictate product̲s̲ ̲ ̲ ̲ ̲ ̲ ̲ ̲ ̲ ̲ ̲) their suppliers. Wal-Mart made retail the dom̲ ̲ ̲ ̲ ̲ ̲ ̲ ̲ ̲ ̲ ̲ ̲ :conomy and the company's power translates int̲ ̲ ̲ ̲ ̲ ̲ ̲ ̲ ̲ ̲ nbined net worth of over \$100 billion, the Walto̲ ̲ ̲ ̲ ̲ ̲ ̲ ̲ ̲ ̲ ilies in the world. Depending on the current val̲ ̲ ̲ ̲ ̲ ̲ ̲ ̲ ̲ t three of the ten wealthiest Americans [www.forb̲ ̲ ̲ ̲ ̲ ̲ ̲ ̲ ̲ ons. The magnetic field generated by the compan̲ ̲ ̲ ̲ ̲ ̲ ̲ ̲ orthwest Arkansas from a sleepy rural region into a growing ̲ ̲ ̲ ̲ ̲ ea as hundreds of vendors established permanent offices near the company headquarters.

Wal-Mart is surrounded by an aura of normalcy. Through public relations, advertising, and décor, Wal-Mart presents itself as a proud embodiment of American patriotism, democracy, Christian family values, consumer choice, and free market principles. With the possible exception of McDonald's, no other business represents America like Wal-Mart. In a poll conducted by Vanity Fair in 2009, 48 percent of the respondents indicated that Wal-Mart "best symbolizes America today."[1] Despite their unprecedented success (or rather precisely because of it), Wal-Mart is at the center of American and global political and moral debates. More than any other company, Wal-Mart incites ambivalence: optimism, reassurance, and genuine consumer satisfaction come alongside repulsion, anger, and even loathing (Dicker 2005). The company appears as both a boon to shoppers that is vitally necessary and central to the American way of life, and as the worst threat to it. In a 2005 survey, respondents ranked Wal-Mart second only to Enron when asked about which company they trusted the least. But in the very same survey, Wal-Mart scored second only to General Electric as the most trusted (Serwer 2005).

"Shopping at Wal-Mart isn't an innocent experience" writes investigative journalist Charles Fishman, author of the best-selling book *The Wal-Mart Effect* (2005): "It is a mix of satisfaction, wonder, puzzlement, and guilt. The nagging feeling, of course, is its own hidden cost, unaccounted for" (200). Fishman cites an intriguing study conducted by an ad agency in Oklahoma which found that shoppers with "conflicted" attitudes toward Wal-Mart spent three times as much money in the store as the shoppers who were labeled "enthusiasts"; "conflicted" shoppers also visited the store more frequently, nearly six times as often as any other group (220). Many Americans are ambivalent toward Wal-Mart, even as low prices pull them back as customers.

All of these features—its size   ss, its symbolic
connection to America, and the   ngs it incites—
make Wal-Mart an important an   ological study.
The controversies surrounding Wa   rasting currents
in American society. Indeed, it i   to disentangle
criticisms of Wal-Mart from those leveled at corporate America and the global
economy more generally, and it is certainly misleading and unfair to single
out Wal-Mart as the exception to the rule. However, many of these criticisms
are crystallized by Wal-Mart's unprecedented success, its sheer size and power,
their vanguard role in the industry, in addition to their innovative, and generally
effective, responses to critics.

Defamiliarizing Wal-Mart

One of the aims of this book is to introduce readers to some of cultural
anthropology's [http://en.wikipedia.org/wiki/Cultural_anthropology] basic
concepts and to demonstrate their usefulness by applying them to Wal-Mart.
Anthropologists use the concepts of normalization and naturalization to refer
to the processes through which ideas, behaviors and social arrangements—
such as Wal-Mart's inexorable growth or global capitalism—come to appear
ordinary, unquestioned, and inevitable—as if they had a life of their own.
Rather than take the ordinary for granted, anthropologists regards the normal
as strange, and think of becoming normal as an achievement, or an effect of
cultural work. Turning the anthropological gaze, typically associated with
"exotic" others, toward the taken for granted world demonstrates its construct-
edness, its arbitrariness toward the taken-for-granted world, its unintended
consequences, and the possibility that things could be otherwise. One method
of defamiliarization examines the conditions and processes through which the
objects, practices, meanings, feelings, and forms of social life that we take for
granted came into existence; it aims "to provoke attention to the forces that
come into view as habit or shock, resonance or impact" (Stewart 2007, 1).
When we reconstruct the conditions of possibility of the present, we appreciate
the assembled and constructed nature of the social worlds we inhabit. This
book attempts to denaturalize Wal-Mart, and American society by extension,
by examining its culturally constructed nature.

Wal-Mart is both a product and a producer of American society, and a
producer of it. Understanding the forces behind Wal-Mart's much heralded
expansion reveals a great deal about the shifting social, political, and economic
landscape. Exploring their corporate culture and practices also draws our
attention toward the ways that the mega-corporation is actively reshaping the
conditions under which we live, whether we shop there or not. By training

our attention on Wal-Mart's many paradoxes and controversies, we hope to illuminate contradictions deep within the American Dream itself and to explore alternatives.

This book examines the conditions of possibility for Wal-Mart as well as its social effects. A central theme of this book is that Wal-Mart's success is directly related to its adaptability to a regulatory environment that privileges efficiency and profit maximization above all else, and to its corresponding ability to capitalize on the failure of American society (and societies around the world) to make the Dream attainable for a significant number of its citizens. Wal-Mart's simple yet compelling response to this failure has been to make the material trappings of the Dream cheaper, in price and quality, and more conveniently located.

Another central focus of this book is how Wal-Mart manages negative externalities, the transaction costs borne by the general public. Low costs and convenience have generated numerous social and environmental consequences. Many of which were neither readily apparent to, nor understood to be relevant by, Wal-Mart proponents or shoppers, but became increasingly difficult to ignore as Wal-Mart grew. Many Americans blame Wal-Mart for filling our lives and landfills with piles of plastic junk, for lowering wages and eliminating jobs, and for destroying small town America, and the vibrant forms of public and civic life that are nostalgically associated with it. A chorus of critics asserts that Wal-Mart has grown powerful enough to constitute a serious threat to democracy.

Such unintended consequences fuel Americans' ambivalence toward Wal-Mart. These side effects have engendered a variety of criticisms and even some organized and effective forms of resistance. In response, Wal-Mart has mounted a permanent public relations blitz, always emp   de for customers and employees. They have also   ess practices, most recently by adopting ambitious e   ite sustained opposition, Wal-Mart has shown a   its externalities, fend off unions, avoid major law   ns, and expand into new towns and countries.

In order to understand how Wal-Mart accom   ht several revolutionary aspects of their approach. The first regards how Wal-Mart has tied its success to its ability to deliver low prices to consumers, such that these consumers benefit directly from the externalities associated with cutting costs. Second, Wal-Mart fosters real experiences of satisfaction, inclusion, social mobility, and fulfillment, for both shoppers and employees within this imagined world. Third, Wal-Mart has worked to elaborate a plausible worldview in which the company, its business practices, and the regulatory framework that allows it to operate are depicted and perceived as beneficial, benign,

ordinary, and inevitable. They strive to present a world in which contradictions
and externalities do not exist. Finally, Wal-Mart invests a considerable amount
of time and creative energy positioning itself as a free market solution to social
problems, such as poverty, inequality, and environmental destruction. Indeed,
Wal-Mart claims to solve the very problems that it is accused of creating, while
alternative solutions, especially labor unions or regulatory changes, are dis-
qualified as unnecessary or harmful.

Despite these effective strategies, Wal-Mart has not been able to completely
legitimize itself in the eyes of the public. This is because the problems their
critics highlight are often intrinsic to both contemporary society and the regulatory environment. Wal-Mart insists that they are no different than any other
corporation, and that their business model is both legal and uniquely beneficial.
We contend that popular ambivalence toward Wal-Mart emanates from the
contradictory nature of the American Dream, and the ways that the Dream
has been redefined in the last few decades, including by Wal-Mart itself.

Contradictions at the Heart of the American Dream

Although there is no single characteristic shared by all Americans, there is a
magnetizing narrative and imaginary world to which many people—official
and unofficial Americans alike—relate, and to which they attach their desires:
the American Dream. This imaginary provides both structure and meaning to
our life trajectories, and it encompasses many of the hopes that we prioritize
and strive toward. The American Dream is one of prosperity and inclusion.
It exudes an optimistic attitude and perceives an abundant future and limitless
possibilities. This dream typically positions the nuclear family—imagined as
a source of love, morality and emotional strength—at its center, surrounded
by an evolving assortment of consumer goods. It also includes meaningful
work, and income sufficient to keep members of one's family comfortable,
safe, educated, and well-positioned to live their own version of the Dream.
Also central to the Dream are political values: freedom of speech and of
religion, the freedom to assemble, and the equal opportunity to elect a
representative government. The American Dream is one of individual and
collective achievement, of innovation and creativity. It encapsulates what many
Americans mean by the word freedom, the quality that many believe makes
America both great and unique.

The contemporary version of the Dream was forged in the years following
World War II, when thousands of soldiers returned home, got married, had
children, purchased homes, and found stable careers—often in America's then-
dominant manufacturing sector—and shopped in new discount and five and
dime stores. Many Americans imagine this Dream as unchanging, universal,

and open to everyone. Carried by mass media, American corporations, and international development organizations, the American Dream has become a globally circulating imaginary. American history contains a series of clashes over the specific content of the Dream: how best to achieve it and who the Dream was meant to include. Working and formerly enslaved people, women, immigrants, gay men, and lesbians have fought for access to the Dream (which was often built on their backs), as have people in the formerly colonized world.

There are contradictory currents at the heart of the Dream. The majority of Americans identify strongly with the values of individualism, hard work, and self-reliance. Many Americans believe in a vision of society as a level playing field where competition brings out the best, and where the government is small and stays out of individual lives. They also share a faith in free market capitalism, which many see as the economic system most consistent with an inherently self-interested human nature, and therefore as the ideal system for promoting freedom and happiness. Many believe that wealthier individuals and countries earned and deserve what they have, a belief that celebrates America's exceptionalism and that places wealthy tycoons, inventors, and entrepreneurs like Bill Gates, Donald Trump, and Oprah Winfrey at the top of our pantheon of national icons. Americans display status through consumption—the ability to consume in quantity *and* quality is integral to many Americans' definition of freedom.

Alongside these beliefs, Americans also believe strongly in democracy, equality, fairness, basic standards of human dignity, rights, cooperation, environmental preservation, and moderation—a set of values often at odds with competitive individualism and market logics. This second tendency is most clearly expressed in the social movements of marginalized groups, and had its fullest institutional expression during the New Deal [www.pbs.org/wgbh/americanexperience/features/general-article/dustbowl-new-deal/]. In response to collective political demands, the federal government instituted worker protections, such as minimum wage and pro-union legislation, and established a social safety net, including Social Security and unemployment insurance. The Civil Rights movement fought to extend these programs to non-whites, and they were expanded during LBJ's Great Society, which created Medicare and Medicaid. While these programs never resolved American poverty and inequality, they eased the suffering of millions.

These intertwined legacies of the American Dream exist in tension. Progressives see stark differences between the ethic of mutual care and inclusivity, and a culture of aggressive capitalist competition that promotes an "every person for themselves" mentality. Conservatives, in turn, decry an expensive and wasteful "nanny state" that saps the impulse for freedom, and see the mobilization of excluded groups as threats to the social order. At a deeper level, desires for upward mobility, leisure, and "the good life" often conflict with the demands of work, and an increasing dependence on cheap groceries and consumer goods complicates the desire for fair working conditions, a living wage, healthy lifestyles, and environmental preservation. Americans' faith in deregulated free markets also conflicts with their desire to preserve the local flavor of their most treasured spaces, and the patriotic urge to keep jobs at home.

The American Dream restlessly incorporates these contradictory impulses, and decades of unprecedented prosperity and global superpower status allowed most middle class white Americans to gloss over these divergences. Today, however, there is a widespread sense across the political spectrum that the Dream is threatened by powerful forces that have placed it out of reach for current and future generations. We join many others who suggest that much of this contemporary discontent is related to a new dominant framework of global free market capitalism that has brought the unresolved contradictions at the heart of the Dream to the surface.

The Neoliberal Revolution

American social and economic policy over the last four decades has been heavily tilted toward promoting individualism and free markets, resulting in the steady dismantling of New Deal policies and programs. Neoliberalism is an umbrella term for a governing philosophy that promises economic growth and prosperity through the removal of government from social and economic life: reduced social services and governmental investment, deregulation of businesses and finance, reduced legal protections for organized labor, and lower tax rates for corporations and the wealthy. Neoliberals espouse fiscal austerity and for-profit provision of public services, like education and health care, and prefer global free trade and non-unionized workforces. As an alternative to welfare, they argue that scaling back government programs will stimulate competitive self-interest and mitigate inequality. In an imagined neoliberal utopia, people would rely not on the government, but on a privatized social sphere, run by free market principles that gain their validity through consumer and worker "free choice." Neoliberal deregulation has allowed corporations to outsource manufacturing and strengthened the hand of management against unions. Free marketeers believe that prosperity will emerge when capital is unregulated and able to move freely across the globe. Republicans have espoused neoliberal ideas since the 1960s, and they have been generally embraced by both parties since the Clinton administration. Although neoliberalism is associated with all of these elements, they frequently appear independently, and the actual operation of the "free" market is often at odds with this theory.

An important part of the story of the rise of free market logic is the shareholder value revolution. In *Liquidated: An Ethnography of Wall Street* (2009), Karen Ho describes a transformation in the reason for being of corporations since the 1940s. In the post WWII moment, corporations were understood as having a significant social role as the preeminent social institution of capitalist society, and their health was measured according to their effects on a wide number of shareholders. They were expected to play a role in social cohesion by employing large numbers of people and by promoting general well-being. In subsequent decades, however, Wall Street bankers, through the corporate takeover and restructuring movement that began in the 1990s, imposed a specific conception of shareholder value as the sole metric by which corporate success was to be measured. Shareholder value was maximized by cutting costs, primarily by eliminating waste and "excessive" employment. CEO bonuses were tied to their success in downsizing and outsourcing jobs.

Neoliberal free market policies have made the rich much richer while placing the American Dream increasingly outside the reach of many Americans (Harvey 2007; Reich 2010; Stiglitz 2012), especially women and minority groups [www.mariko-chang.com/LiftingAsWeClimb.pdf] (Duggan 2003). Economic inequality has been growing since the 1970s, as wages have stagnated due to the outsourcing of manufacturing, new automated production technologies, and declining union membership and strength. The politics of budget cutting and self-reliance have taken their toll on community development, public health, education, and the social safety net upon which many Americans rely. In 2008, facilitated largely by the neoliberal dismantling of financial regulations, the collapse of the U.S. housing bubble precipitated a global financial meltdown, leading to massive taxpayer bailouts of banks, and the worst economic recession since the Great Depression. Unemployment soared and millions of Americans have lost their homes, cars, health insurance, businesses, and access to credit. Many poor nations were affected even worse and minority communities in the U.S. were among the hardest hit [www.nationaljournal.com/thenextamerica/economy/recession-impact-minorities-net-worth-falls-by-a-third-20120613]. With poverty and inequality on the rise, Wall Street bankers and investors reaped record profits and evaded criminal prosecution.

Not surprisingly, many Americans have become angry, dispirited, and fearful about the state of the country and the ability of their divided political system to fix it. Although there is widespread agreement that the American Dream is in crisis, there are very different diagnoses about both the nature of the threat and the most appropriate solutions. Democrats cautiously propose new taxes and regulations while Republicans blame taxation and governmental intervention. This division belies overwhelming similarities in their definitions of the problems and their proposed solutions, with neither suggesting that core elements of Dream or of neoliberal policies might be the problem. Most Americans' political beliefs do not fit neatly into "conservative" or "liberal" camps, and polls consistently show strong disapproval of both major political parties. National polls also reflect the fundamental ambivalences with which many Americans struggle but rarely articulate. For example, although majorities often support tax cuts and oppose "big government," many of the same people support effective government programs.[2] Though most are unaware, many are caught between the counter-currents of the Dream, erratically pulled in opposite directions as they seek relief for their individual situations.

The Politics of Wal-Mart's Culture

Wal-Mart's culture is an exceptionally useful site from which to examine contemporary redefinitions of the American Dream. Wal-Mart does not just exist: it is produced by its employees—who run supply chains, stock the shelves, and operate cash registers—as well as by the customers who shop there. Wal-Mart is a multi-sited construction—a complex and highly orchestrated assemblage of bodies, knowledge, practices, feelings, materials, and spaces in constant process of becoming, articulation, and adaptation. Wal-Mart is deliberately and self-consciously constructed through advertising, public relations, and official corporate policies, practices, and traditions that aim to attract shoppers and maintain a harmonious and productive workforce. Wal-Mart's culture is political in the sense that it stakes out some very clear positions on the meaning, content, and inclusivity of the Dream; it attempts to do business in a very particular way, and the company regularly supports specific political causes and candidates. This cultural politics is also evident in their diagnoses of the threats facing the American Dream and in the kinds of solutions they prescribe.

Wal-Mart celebrates a specific set of principles and practices that it refers to as its "culture" [www.walmartstores.com/AboutUs/295.aspx]. Featured prominently on their corporate website, Wal-Mart's culture is comprised of nine essential elements, including: an Open Door policy, through which employees can access management; a set of "rules" governing employee–customer contact; a "grassroots process," that encourages listening to everyone's ideas; the beliefs and practices of "servant leadership"; and a formalized rendering of the company's "three basic beliefs and values"—respect for the individual, service to their customers, and striving for excellence.[3] Wal-Mart also actively cultivates a body of employees and managers that share the core ideologies of the company.

We are interested in Wal-Mart's use and promotion of the concept of a culture, as it codifies official rules and expectations for membership, behavior, and "belonging" in the Wal-Mart world; for enthusiasts, this is much of what makes the company special and unique. Living in Northwest Arkansas, we have heard many employees who believe in the company describe themselves as "drinking the Wal-Mart Kool-aid." However, Wal-Mart's culture extends far beyond these nine elements, many of which are vague ideals and not always practiced. In addition to these and other explicitly stated forms, we are also interested in the understandings that usually go unacknowledged and un-remarked upon, but that are nonetheless embedded assumptions in the actual business practices of the company.

One central aspect of Wal-Mart's culture, exhaustively analyzed in numerous memoirs and management books, is its exacting commitment to thrift and efficiency. Wal-Mart delivers the absolute lowest prices, and thus generates high volume sales, by running an efficient supply chain, squeezing vendors and manufacturers, and keeping labor costs down. Wal-Mart was a vanguard in creating a new world of retail, due to their unique business model and to numerous innovations Sam Walton and his lieutenants adopted in supply chain efficiency and low operating costs (Fishman 2005; Lichtenstein 2009). Wal-Mart narrates their success as a revolutionary victory for consumers. Wal-Mart ranges from thrifty to stingy and elevates saving money for consumers into an almost sacred goal—a bottom line that cannot be compromised. More than any other aspect of Wal-Mart culture, these efficiencies explain Wal-Mart's meteoric rise and competitive dominance.

Also central to Wal-Mart's culture is its incessant self-promotion as normal, ordinary, beneficial, and inevitable. The company emits a relentless optimism about itself and the world, emblematized by its former "smiley face" logo, as well as its replacement, "the spark." "[C]arefully disguised as something ordinary, familiar and prosaic" (Fishman 2005, 221), Wal-Mart simultaneously presents itself as exceptional, heroic, and larger than life, as a living example of the kind of spirit that makes America exceptional. It is at once corny, home-spun, simple, gigantic, astonishing and awe-inspiring. It is an earnest, unsophisti-cated, superhero—a cross between Forrest Gump and Superman. Wal-Mart celebrates its identity as a defender of consumer interest, an engine of share-holder value, and as an inclusive family for its millions of associates. Wrapped in the flag, it marks itself as sentimentally patriotic. It typically cultivates a Southern, Christian, arguably white, self-image and speaks in defense of conservative family values. It can, however, downplay this image when necessary, and the company is increasingly "multicultural" in its operations.

In general, Wal-Mart aggressively asserts the reality, reasonability, universality, and attainability of the American Dream, not least of all through its portrayal of the company's famous founder, Sam Walton. Most visibly dramatized at the Wal-Mart Visitor Center [www.walmartstores.com/AboutUs/287.aspx] in Bentonville, Arkansas, Walton is seen as a kind and humble man who took advantage of the opportunities made possible by American society, the kind of life available to any individual with the right motivation and "spark." Wal-Mart promotes his success story as an affirmation of American values, and as the ultimate horizon of human possibility.

Wal-Mart's official self-representation, corporate practices, and philanthropy reinforce a collective vision in which the divergent tendencies of the American Dream coexist without conflict or contradiction. Wal-Mart presents global free market capitalism and consumer culture as perfectly—even intrinsically—compatible with American values of democracy, equality, freedom, and fairness, as well as with the ideals of Christian morality and responsible environmental stewardship. As we demonstrate in the following chapters, the retailer promises utopia to the citizens of the world, many of who are struggling to make ends meet. We show that these are not empty ideals. Rather, they constitute an integrated worldview shared by many Wal-Mart managers, employees, and customers. They are also not simply representations; Wal-Mart fosters concrete lived experiences of satisfaction, social mobility, equality, dignity, multicultural inclusion, access, and patriotism.

Wal-Mart and the American Dream

A product of its emergence in the rural Ozarks, the management philosophies and techniques of its founding leaders, and circumstance, Wal-Mart's combination of efficiency and low prices excelled in a corporate world ruled by shareholder value, and a social world characterized by a shrinking middle class and rising inequality. Wal-Mart's revolutionary innovation lies not only in its efficiency, but in the way that it ties the goal of shareholder value to the provision of low prices for customers. Its business model presents these two core values as inextricably linked, turning customers into de facto stakeholders. Wal-Mart's associates who became millionaires as stock prices skyrocketed is a recurring piece of company folklore. Even when the goal of shareholder value trades off with the material interests of many stakeholders (e.g., employees, suppliers, the community, etc.), these effects are arguably offset by cost savings.

Equally revolutionary are the ways that Wal-Mart has been able to include a large number of customers and employees as "affective stakeholders": people who feel a sense of belonging to the company—even as critics fault the company for destroying communities. Wal-Mart's low prices allow millions of American shoppers, including the downwardly mobile, to experience satisfaction and feel more in control of their financial lives. Many employees feel like members of the "Wal-Mart family" and experience themselves as on a path to success. What is interesting is how these forms of emotional and symbolic inclusion emerged as previous conceptions of stakeholder rights, and the jobs and social cohesion that they supported, were disappearing in the economy at large, and as the possibilities for social mobility were shrinking, not expanding. Wal-Mart makes economic stagnation and downturns more livable for individuals and families by offering a vision of the American Dream that fits into their increasingly cramped economic—and physical—confines. This promise is encapsulated in the aspirational model of social mobility for which they are now famous: *Save Money. Live Better.* This story narrates Wal-Mart as a hero for low income, ordinary, and aspiring Americans, a tale that has become a lived experience for millions of Wal-Mart's customers and employees.

Lauren Berlant (2011) describes a condition of "cruel optimism" when "the object that draws your attachment actively impedes the aim that brought you to it" (1). She relates this condition to the ways that we remain in the thrall of dreams of prosperity that have been placed increasingly out of reach by neoliberal restructuring. How is our optimism replenished, despite its constant frustration? We argue that Wal-Mart is actively engaged at many levels in a reconfiguration of the material, conceptual, and affective production of the Dream to make its shriveling less visible and more tolerable to excluded groups. Wal-Mart works, by accident and by design, for profit and PR, to smooth out the rough edges of life in the neoliberal world, to distract us from its profound contradictions, and to ameliorate our suffering while at the same time working to reinforce the conditions under which we are systematically subjected to harm.

Wal-Mart's solution to the contradictions of the American Dream draws heavily on neoliberal thought. Wal-Mart presents itself as a private sphere alternative to progressive efforts to include marginalized groups in the Dream and to protect the environment. Wal-Mart frames Americans' and the world's economic problems not in terms of structural contradictions between market logics and human needs, but in terms of lack of access to low price consumer goods and lack of opportunities for individual mobility through hard work— two things that Wal-Mart claims to provide. Wal-Mart's solution treats social inequalities—between men and women, whites and non-whites, rich and poor, "first" and "third" worlds—as simply existing, rather than as the product of historical and contemporary forms of sexism, racism, and colonialism. Wal-Mart actively reinforces these structural asymmetries because their business model relies on a poor and disorganized labor force willing to work for low wages as well as on structural inequalities between countries. The company treats environmental destruction as potentially resolved by green consumerism, rather than integral to an economic system based on perpetual economic growth, and their own low price business model.

Wal-Mart's revolutionary approach—linking shareholder value to "Everyday Low Prices" (EDLP), promoting affective inclusion for customers and employees, conjuring visions of a conflict free social life, and positioning itself as a free market solution to social problems—has helped the company fend off regulation and unions, normalize their externalities, and justify their labor policies and sourcing practices. These revolutionary innovations give moral force to Wal-Mart's formidable public relations and political efforts. At a broader level, their model helps to normalize and legitimate the neoliberal regulatory framework itself. In short, through shopping or working at Wal-Mart (and its imitators) we become stakeholders in the liquidation of the American dream.

The cultural politics of Wal-Mart reflect broader trends on the American political landscape. Wal-Mart's success parallels the rightward shift in American politics, and their meteoric rise as a company paralleled the Republican Party's success in rural America since the 1980s (Lichtenstein 2009). Many liberals question why white, working class voters who historically supported unions and public investment now seem to ignore their economic interests in favor of conservative Republican candidates and neoliberal agendas. According to Thomas Frank, author of *What's the Matter with Kansas?* (2004), modern conservatives have pursued a right wing economic agenda by catering to the cultural issues—such as school prayer, second amendment rights, and abortion—that are important to working class, rural, white, Christians, especially in the South. Although Frank suggests that conservatives choose between their values and their pocketbooks, Wal-Mart's low price model blunts the blow of neoliberal policies, while their corporate culture elaborates a world in which Christian family values and free market capitalism are entirely consistent (Moreton 2009). The challenge currently facing Wal-Mart is how to reproduce their remarkable success in blue states, urban areas, and foreign countries, each with different regulatory frameworks and definitions of the good life.

Wal-Mart and its Critics

What happens when low prices and shareholder value are not enough, or when the drive to achieve them generates new problems? What about the Wal-Mart hourly employees who find themselves unable to make ends meet, much less climb the ladder? What happens when the forms of symbolic and affective belonging run into the cold realities of efficiency and the bottom line? If much of our contemporary dissatisfaction is rooted in asymmetrical socio-economic structures and neoliberal frameworks that Wal-Mart leaves largely unchanged, and even works to reinforce, what other solutions are possible? To explore these questions, we turn to anti-Wal-Mart culture and the alternatives that they propose.

Anti-Wal-Mart culture is diverse and not free of contradictions. There are at least three main tendencies within anti-Wal-Mart culture, each of which can be found independently or in combination. The first tendency could be described as elitists, snobs, and "haters": these critics simply dismiss Wal-Mart and its customers as trashy and low class, and see their stores as eyesores. Such criticisms invariably strengthen the company's image as a democratic space where everyone is treated with respect. The second group consists of those who single out Wal-Mart unfairly, treating it as an exception to the rule, and who thereby fail to see its fundamental similarities to other businesses. These critics take for granted the neoliberal political and economic order that allows Wal-Mart and others like it to thrive. Elitist anti-Wal-Mart critics typically do not describe alternative ways to include the people whose concrete and pressing needs for products and employment are met, albeit partially, by Wal-Mart. The solutions proposed by the second group tend to be based in a nostalgic idea about how capitalism works that bears little relation to contemporary reality. Were the company to suddenly disappear, one or several big box clones would rush to fill what would be a substantial void on the retail landscape.

Although Wal-Mart dismisses the majority of their critics as "Wal-Mart haters" or as "liberal elites" who are loath to appreciate the success of a Southern, Christian, conservative company, this caricature does not describe all of its opponents. The third group of anti-Wal-Mart critics sees Wal-Mart's success as a symptom of a corporate friendly regulatory framework and an increasingly unequal national and global economic system—the post 1970s neoliberal economic and political realities. These groups suggest a change in the regulatory framework and in social inequality itself as an alternative to Wal-Mart, at least in the way that the company is currently configured.

While there is considerable variation within this final group of critics, they tend to see the problems of poverty, unemployment, and lack of access to food and resources as structural products of a larger economic system, and they look for solutions at that level. Many of these critics propose or enact a rethinking of the American Dream in a way that is more egalitarian, less commodified, and far less environmentally destructive. Some of these critics promote a model of human rights that includes a set of basic protections for all, including worker safety and dignity, regardless of race, class, gender, level of education, or national origin. Several critics contend that Wal-Mart's size and hard knuckle tactics subvert true free market principles. Some of these critics remind us that poverty and wealth are deeply intertwined. They encourage us to connect the dots in the global chains of production and consumption, and to examine the social costs that these connections produce. They encourage us to see that many of the problems associated with Wal-Mart stem from an economy based on perpetual economic growth, and they ask us to consider the extent to which our "American" desires for equality, global development, environmental protection, and meaningful work might be incompatible with an unregulated free market and a culture of unchecked consumerism. Unlike Wal-Mart, which enjoys an aura of normalcy, these critics are often seen as dreamers or radicals. From our perspective, it is difficult to see why their ideas are any more radical than Wal-Mart's.

The chapters in this book focus on the paradoxes and controversies surrounding Wal-Mart. They aim to illuminate contradictions deep within the American Dream, and call attention to existing and imagined alternatives. This book intends to provoke reflection on the very foundations of the American Dream and how it might be reconfigured in a more democratic, inclusive, and sustainable way. What is at stake in the disputes surrounding Wal-Mart is the question of how we can and should constitute social and political life for this and future generations. We are motivated by the knowledge that, because we collectively construct the world that makes Wal-Mart possible and in which it has become useful and vital, we can also unmake it, or at the very least, make it differently, in ways that are more harmonious with human and environmental values.

2

FROM THE OZARKS TO
THE PLANET

This chapter tells the story of Wal-Mart's astounding ascent, from a single Five and Dime in Bentonville, Arkansas to the heights of global retail dominance. We examine Wal-Mart's rise in relationship to both a broader history of retail and to transformations in the American economy more generally. Chroniclers of Wal-Mart's growth tend to emphasize the visionary leadership of Sam Walton [www.biographyshelf.com/sam_walton_biography.html]—the self-made, disciplined, and hard-nosed capitalist whose vision the company strives to both adhere to and adapt. Walton is also thought of as a forward-thinking vanguard, due to the numerous innovations in efficiency and information technology he oversaw during his years as CEO. These characterizations are complemented by descriptions of "Mr. Sam" as an unpretentious fellow with a common touch who was dedicated to the needs of his customers and employees. At the 2012 Annual Shareholders' Meeting (ASM), his children called him simply "a merchant with a servant's heart." This narrative has been carefully curated and popularized by Wal-Mart, and forms the basis for the video that greets tourists in the Wal-Mart Visitor Center in Bentonville.

In this chapter, we complicate the "Cult of Sam" with the work of several historians and journalists who have pointed to a number of *other* factors—some accidental, some infrastructural—that contributed to Walton's success: a complicated mix of foresight and individual initiative, shared and stolen ideas, governmental assistance, competitor's mistakes, and the suitability of Wal-Mart's business model to the changing economic realities of the late twentieth century.

Wal-Mart critics multiplied as the company expanded. Many have voiced concerns about the "hidden costs" of Wal-Mart's business model that they feel greatly outweigh the benefits of low prices and consumer convenience. We introduce a range of Wal-Mart's critics, and introduce some of the strategies that Wal-Mart has adopted as it attempts to continue expanding in a rapidly changing world.

The Modern Department Store

A glimpse at what retail shopping was like before Wal-Mart helps us to appreciate what makes the company unique. At the turn of the twentieth century, global manufacturing was in full swing and churning out a large supply of consumables—the fruits of the industrial revolution. How people shopped for these goods depended a great deal on where they lived. In cities, large and elegant department stores housed a great number of consumer goods designed to enhance all aspects of life. In the northeast, some of the bigger names included Macy's, Marshall Fields, and Gimbel's, while the south was home to more regional chains such as Foley's in Texas and Harvey's in Nashville. Clerks guided well-to-do shoppers through a range of fineries, including toys, china, hardware, jewelry, and designer clothing. Department stores—with their seemingly endless supply of goods, pampering clerks, trendy designs, and magical storefront windows designed to awaken shoppers' aspirations—were the birthplace of American consumer culture (Whitaker 2006). They played a significant role, for example, in popularizing the story of Santa Claus in the U.S., helping to turn Christmas into the gift-laden affair of today. These stores functioned as a key social institution in fin de siècle America, and they facilitated the emergence of shopping as both a leisure activity and a predominant mode of self-definition. They were the primary material outfitters of a growing middle class and served, particularly for upper-class women, as a quasi-public sphere (Hilton 2000).

Before the arrival of "discount" stores, rural shoppers gained access to a less refined set of manufactured goods—and the dreams they carried—through giant mail order warehouses, whose extensive, mass distributed catalogues were a virtual compendia of the artifacts of modern life. The leaders in this category were Sears [http://search.ancestry.com/search/db.aspx?dbid=1670&o_iid=46256&o_lid=46256&o_sch=Web+Property] and Montgomery Ward. Both ran highly efficient systems which, combined with low overhead, allowed them to beat their local competition on both price and inventory (Strasser 2006). The spread of urbanization and the rise of the automobile allowed these mail order houses to open their first "brick and mortar" facilities, and chain stores began anchoring shopping centers across suburban America. As the most successful of this group, Sears leveraged their buying power to provide bargain prices on "middle-brand, middle-quality products for the middle-class family" (Lichtenstein 2009, 21).

The Rise of a Rural Chain Store

Sam Walton married Helen Robson in 1943 and purchased his first business in 1945—a Ben Franklin variety store in Newport, Arkansas. In order to make the $25,000 down payment, Sam borrowed $20,000 from Helen's father. The store was supplied by Butler Brothers, an industrial distributor that marketed their products through several retail franchise outlets. Sam made his store a success by keeping prices as low as his agreement with Butler Brothers allowed. Walton well understood the importance of low prices in mid-1940's Arkansas; He was preoccupied with making his products more available to poor rural people, many of who were struggling with an economic malaise that had changed little since the great Depression (Lichtenstein 2009, 25; also Bianco 2006; Moreton 2009), but his franchise agreement gave him little leeway to do so.

Despite his success, Walton lost his lease in 1950 when the property owner rented the business to his son. Unwilling to work for another retailer, Sam relocated his family to Bentonville, Arkansas, where he purchased another Ben Franklin, the first of a chain that he would soon open in southern Missouri and Kansas. One of these, which opened in 1951 on the Bentonville Town Square (and now serves as the company's official Visitor Center) was named "Walton's Five and Dime" (see Figure 2.1); the first official Wal-Mart opened down the road in Rogers in 1962. During these years, Walton worked long hours to master the art of discount merchandising and borrowed liberally from his competition. He was an early adopter of the self-serve model that, because it allowed customers to create their own paths through the store, led to increased sales. It also allowed Walton to cut labor costs: placing just a few cash registers at the front of the store, rather than one in each department, made it possible to hire fewer employees who needed less training (Lichtenstein 2009, 32; also Bianco 2006, 44–45). Although low wages were common in chain stores at the time (Strasser 2006), Walton made this the bedrock of his business model.

Despite these cost-saving innovations, Walton's efforts to lower prices were blocked. His franchise agreement, which required that he stock 80 percent of his shelves with Butler Brothers products, limited his ability to stock many discounted items. The second obstacle was the Robinson-Patman Act [www.ftc. gov/speeches/other/patman.shtm], passed in 1936, which, in an attempt to protect "mom and pop" stores from chains like Ben Franklin, stipulated that all merchants sell their goods at the manufacturers' suggested price. Though he broke the law when he could (and its enforcement gradually waned as a result of industry pressure), Sam Walton still faced the same problem confronted by chain store retailers throughout the United States: a cumbersome, inefficient, and costly supply chain that was filled with middlemen and had improved little since the turn of the century (Drucker 1972; Lichtenstein 2009, 33).

Walton became an avid student of other retail innovators who were devising creative ways to cut costs. One of these was Eugene Ferkauf, a New Yorker who tried to outmaneuver the Robinson-Patman act by creating a member's

Figure 2.1 The Wal-Mart Visitor Center in Bentonville, Arkansas. Home to Sam Walton's
original Five and Dime.

only, self-service store known as E.J. Korvette. Ferkauf sold high volumes of
top-selling branded items by significantly marking down their prices, and in
1952, he opened a second store on Long Island. Walton also studied Kmart,
the Detroit-based discounter that catered to bargain hunting working-class
shoppers in America's growing suburbs. Kmart had only one entrance and
exit, all the registers were at the front of the store, and they sold a variety of
non-branded items that were manufactured overseas. With these techniques,
Kmart was beating Walton at a game that he had not yet been able to play:
offering low prices and self-service shopping to cash-strapped but aspirational
consumers. During the 1960s, Sam watched Kmart stores spread like wildfire
throughout the United States.

A bank loan eventually allowed Walton to purchase in volume, expand his
stores, and then to build his own warehouse and distribution center (DC)
[www.walmartstores.com/AboutUs/7794.aspx] in Bentonville in 1970. Arguably
the first innovation that can be credited to Walton himself, the DC allowed
him to buy in bulk at the lowest possible price. Perhaps even more importantly,
it also allowed him to eliminate the "middlemen," the distributors who raised
prices and controlled the delivery schedule.

Walton immediately passed these savings on to his customers, counting on high volume sales to recoup his investment. He opened several Wal-Mart stores over the course of a few years, quickly adding to his collection throughout the region that he referred to as his "magic circle." Walton grew carefully, making sure that all of his stores were serviceable by Wal-Mart's own expanding supply chain; stores multiplied in relationship to distribution centers. Significantly, the DCs were not built as warehouses but rather as high-tech processing centers, operating under a "continuous replenishment model" that facilitated the efficient delivery of products to nearby stores (Blanchard et al. 2008).

But what was so magic about Sam Walton's circle? Several regional factors contributed to Wal-Mart's early expansion. The first was a recently dislocated workforce that was primarily female, did not demand higher wages, and was less familiar with unions. Second, the local competition of family-run stores was still grappling with the problems that Walton had recently surmounted: small and externally-controlled inventories and their associated higher costs. Once rural populations began driving more regularly, they were no longer a captive audience for these establishments. Third, Walton built stores in county seats: towns small enough that he could extract tax breaks and other financial subsidies, but big enough to draw shoppers from surrounding areas. Fourth, Sam Walton followed government contracts—the postwar years saw a rapid rise in military spending in rural areas throughout the Sun Belt south (Moreton 2009). Possibly drawing on his experience of working for a military contractor in Oklahoma, Walton established many of his early stores near bases and weapons plants, where his stores served a sizable number of employed working class customers.

Through a combination of business acumen, luck, borrowed money, and hard work, Sam Walton broke through a once-imposing set of structural barriers and soon began to outpace his competitors. Walton opened over 500 new stores in the 1970s and, by the end of the decade he was one of the largest retailers in the country. And though the 1970s were marked by "stagflation," a combination of stubborn inflation and depressed wages, historian Nelson Lichtenstein (2009) suggests that Walton's small town expansion strategy enabled him to avoid the economic crunch in urban areas and stay afloat (42).

When the Federal Reserve raised interest rates in the early 1980s, many of Walton's competitors were deeply in debt and reliant on an outsourced and expensive supply chain. Wal-Mart, in contrast, was attractive to investors, had excellent credit, and was poised for expansion. The company's logistical innovations and investments had paid off: because of their stripped-down operating costs, they could offer rock-bottom prices to an increasingly frugal customer base. Unlike Sears, who mistakenly assumed that "the American middle class would enlarge itself indefinitely" (Lichtenstein 2009, 21), Wal-Mart was keenly focused on the basic needs of low income consumers.

By the early 1980s, Wal-Mart had effectively linked high profits with low prices and they were selling in record volume. This business model was generating unprecedented profits for both management and stockholders, and the company was celebrated as the apex of management science (Lichtenstein 2009, 44–45). In 1984, Walton bet future CEO David Glass that they could not earn a pre-tax profit margin of more than 8 percent, and hula danced down Wall Street [www.walmartstores.com/AboutUs/293.aspx] when he lost. This kind of hokey behavior embellished his image as a humble and corny tycoon.

The Wal-Mart Effect

In his autobiography *Made in America*, Sam Walton admits to being cheap:

> In the beginning, I was so chintzy I really didn't pay my employees well. It wasn't that I was intentionally heartless, I was so obsessed with turning in a profit margin of 6 percent or higher that I ignored some of the basic needs of our people, and I feel bad about it
>
> (1993, 127–128)

Walton's thrift was legendary and it remains a central feature of the company's success. Their refusal to increase wages, the hours they "squeeze" out of their associates, forcing executives to share hotel rooms on business trips, and their early and unwavering commitment to global outsourcing are just a few of the ways that Wal-Mart maintains the "Everyday Low Costs" (EDLC) that they insist are integral to their low prices. In this context, Walton's expression of remorse is striking in that it undermines the company's self-image as a path to social mobility. If even Mr. Sam was conflicted about low wages, how should the rest of us feel?

An important historical factor that played a vital role in Wal-Mart's ascendancy in the early 1980s was the "shareholder value revolution" that Karen Ho describes in her ethnography *Liquidated* (2009). This shift was characterized by "hostile takeovers" of companies by shareholders—usually followed by downsizing and efficiency measures—that were based in the belief that corporations existed solely to generate shareholder profits. Prior to this, workers had been considered core constituents of U.S. corporations whose needs, at times, took precedence over those of financial investors (122–124). Wal-Mart's lean, efficient operation gave them an edge, helping them to both fend off a takeover as well as gain access to cheap credit. Corporations like Sears and Ford, whose workers were either unionized or otherwise protected by generous benefits programs, were forced to dismantle many of these agreements in order to stay competitive (Meyer 1981; Strasser 2006). Fortunately for Sam, his company never had either.

Squeezing Vendors

During the 1970s, Walton was one of the first retailers to invest heavily in computer technology in order to process data from sales, profits, expenses, and inventory that was transmitted daily from each store in his expanding enterprise. This began as a slow, handwritten process, but the innovation of the Universal Price Code (UPC) symbol and the refinement of laser technology allowed point of sale (POS) data to be saved immediately at the checkout counter. UPCs also allowed stores to manage much larger inventories. Walton purchased a satellite to save money processing credit card purchases and to route POS information back to computers in Bentonville. Wal-Mart could now see, in real-time, which products were selling, how quickly, and in what combinations; they now knew more than the manufacturers did about their own products. No one predicted how significant this would be: knowing what products to place alongside one another on the shelves and how much inventory was needed gave Wal-Mart the edge in their relationships with vendors. And, because Wal-Mart now knew exactly how much of a product they had on hand at any given time, they became very precise about ordering. This saved them money as it allowed them to turn the cost of inventory storage back over to their suppliers. Prior to this, manufacturers had used brand recognition, generated by advertising, to dictate purchases, prices, pay schedules, and marketing practices to retailers.

In 1987, in a concession to Wal-Mart's dominance, Procter & Gamble (P&G)—the world's largest packaged goods supplier—struck a deal with the retailer in which the two companies agreed to share information, merge systems, and move to "automatic" or "just in time" ordering and production. P&G also established a permanent office in Bentonville. As Wal-Mart grew, becoming far and away the largest seller of P&G's product lines, Wal-Mart's buyers began to assert even more power over their vendors, now called "partners" in Wal-Mart-speak.

For better or worse, this "just in time" model of managing inventory extended to employees. Although the 1980s saw numerous workers displaced by downsized corporations and outsourced labor, Wal-Mart's tactic was to maximize the efficiency of the ones they had. Enabled by "predictive technology" (Hays 2004), Wal-Mart was now able to staff their stores in relation to traffic and inventory patterns.

Currently, Wal-Mart requires that all their vendors use an in-house information processing program known as Retail Link, a mandate that deepens vendors' connection to and dependence on the company. Retail Link makes it possible for manufacturers to forecast and analyze their products' perform-ance within individual stores, information that can benefit both Wal-Mart and their vendors. Wal-Mart has remained at the forefront of the innovation of data gathering technology in order to better understand, predict, and capitalize on consumer behavior. Beyond Retail Link, they gather Radio Frequency Identification data that tracks each product's movement throughout the store and *@Walmart Labs* [www.walmartlabs.com/], a new ecommerce project, utilizes a program called the Social Genome [http://blogs.smithsonianmag.com/ideas/2011/09/walmart-goes-social/] to mine social networking data to micro-target products to shoppers.

Because most of this data belongs to Wal-Mart, it often forces manufacturers to comply with product-related decisions with which they might not agree. But few complain openly for fear of offending the company. Indeed, Wal-Mart's tremendous buying power, combined with their knowledge advantage, places manufacturers almost at their mercy. This concentration of purchasing power—that economists call a monopsony—gives Wal-Mart near complete control over the retail market. If Wal-Mart doesn't get the price or delivery schedule they want, they can threaten to move elsewhere, potentially devastating the supplier. Fishman calls this powerful and virtually inescapable supply chain ripple—that extends far beyond Wal-Mart—the "Wal-Mart effect."

Fishman describes how Wal-Mart "squeezes" vendors who feel compelled to meet the company's price, even when it seems impossible, unfair (to them or their workers), or environmentally harmful. Wal-Mart's business model is based on high volume sales and very thin profit margins. In exchange for meeting Wal-Mart's exacting standards suppliers obtain high volume orders, long-term contracts, and efficient payment of invoices (Fishman 2005; Blanchard et al. 2008, 173). Wal-Mart's demands are especially taxing on smaller suppliers; observers have chronicled numerous cases of vendors pushed to the brink of bankruptcy. However, vendors big and small take on the risk and challenge of selling to Wal-Mart because they are drawn by the promise of limitless profits.

The harsh reality, as many critics have pointed out, is that meeting Wal-Mart's demands often means firing employees or compromising their well-being, sometimes by cutting corners on their wages, health, and safety. Wal-Mart insists that their practices are customer-driven, and that low prices cannot be achieved without cutting what they view to be waste and inefficiency. Many business analysts laud Wal-Mart for "[p]utting the customer at the forefront of the supply chain" (Blanchard et al. 2008, 168). But for critics, supply chains are also filled with workers, business owners, salespeople, delivery personnel, and other "middlemen" whose jobs Walton is not on record "feeling bad" about eliminating.

One of the primary ways that Wal-Mart delivered low prices was to use foreign suppliers and to pressure their vendors to follow suit. They were long opposed to limitations on imports proposed by labor organizations who were concerned about American jobs. Today, Wal-Mart is the largest single buyer of Chinese products in the world, a fact they tried to hide for some time, by using a shadow purchasing agency (Lichtenstein 2009, 206). Because unions still had a great deal of emotional sway and political clout in the early 1980s, Wal-Mart faced political pressure to change their practices. This led to the store's famous "Buy America" campaign, which assured customers that they would make every effort to sell products manufactured in the United States. The program successfully branded the company as patriotic, despite the fact that foreign imports rose through the 1990s and that Wal-Mart never released any measurable data about its impact. But the lure of low prices was too powerful to ignore, and as American consumers became habituated to lower prices, political opposition to outsourcing waned.

Consolidation and Control

By the mid-1990s, Wal-Mart was the number one retailer in the U.S.; in the 2000s, they also became the country's largest grocer, controlling nearly 23 percent of the national market by 2009, a near-quadruple increase from the 6 percent they controlled in 1998. With total volume sales of almost $150 billion annually, the company doubled the sales of Kroger, their nearest competitor. This growth had a significant impact on agricultural producers, who were now entangled in Wal-Mart's "efficient" supply chain. A 2010 United Food and Commercial Workers' (UFCW) report describes Wal-Mart's impact on the meat industry [www.ufcw.org/docUploads/AG%20Consolidation%20White %20Paper2.pdf?CFID=14068055&CFTOKEN=16463334] and contends that Wal-Mart has used their power as the most important purchaser of agricultural goods to reduce producers' profits, a process that has accelerated the concentration of those industries. Although Wal-Mart did not start this trend, the UFCW holds them accountable for the force of its impact: "there has been no more powerful, and in many cases destructive, presence in this transformed retail landscape than Wal-Mart."

The same pattern exists in other industries. Even though other buyers exist, critics like Barry Lynn (2006) believe that Wal-Mart's buying power is near absolute, concluding that Wal-Mart "does not *participate* in the market so much as use its power to *micromanage* the market, carefully coordinating the actions of thousands of firms from a position *above* the market" (our emphasis). Lynn and co-author Philip Longman (2010) argue that such consolidation leads to a greater concentration of wealth among the top earners within corporations like Wal-Mart, and to fewer resources distributed among the rest of society:

Figure 2.2 Members of the Food Chain Workers Alliance protest in front of a Wal-Mart in Fayetteville, AR during the 2011 ASM.

As behemoth retailers garner ever more power over the sale of some product or service, they also gain an ever greater ability to strip away the profits that once would have made their way into the hands of suppliers. The money that the managers and workers at these smaller companies would have used to expand their businesses, or upgrade their machinery and skills, is instead transferred to the bottom lines of dominant retailers and traders and thence to shareholders.

In this way, consolidation accelerates the upward redistribution of wealth that has placed the American Dream out of reach for millions.

Wal-Mart would counter that their squeeze compensates for this by lowering prices for everyone. To some extent this is true, but savings have not stopped the trend toward rising inequality. Furthermore, Lynn (2006) offers anecdotal evidence that some suppliers end up charging more to other retailers in order to compensate for the razor-thin profits they generate with Wal-Mart. Consolidation also reduces choice for consumers, who now must purchase from companies whose standards have been set by Wal-Mart. It may therefore be naïve for us to say that we "don't shop at Wal-Mart" because the products we purchase elsewhere are likely produced to the company's specifications.

* * *

In effect, we are all caught in Wal-Mart's squeeze. Wal-Mart is the most powerful corporation in human history, and their power extends far beyond the supply chain. They influence how consumers shop and what they desire. They exercise intricate forms of governance over their retail workforce, shaping not only the conditions under which they labor, but also the ways that they feel and think—about the company, about their own lives and interests, and about the possibilities for individual and collective agency. They shape what we all consider to be normal. They are particularly concerned with procuring a cheap labor force, stopping unionization in North America, and limiting worker power in their international stores. In addition, the company deploys a sophisticated set of strategies for entering towns, cities, and foreign countries. Finally, Wal-Mart leverages its size to influence the political systems in all of the countries and localities where it operates, using a variety of mechanisms—some illegal and many nearly invisible—that merit scrutiny. These strategies, the thinking behind them, their effects, and the forms of opposition that they encounter are the focus of this book.

Many believe that corporations have grown too powerful, and that Wal-Mart epitomizes the need for new forms of regulation. Nelson Lichtenstein (2011b) sees a company governed by an authoritarian and sexist culture, and describes how they tyrannically govern over a retail empire and supply chain that exploits vulnerable labor forces all over the world. Barry Lynn views the company as one of a number of "oligopolies" on the corporate landscape that have been allowed to grow unchecked because of President Ronald Reagan's repeal of antitrust legislation in the 1980s. They and others agree that the extreme and unprecedented consolidation taking place across a number of industries (including agribusiness, banking, energy, pharmaceuticals, and health care) has given rise to a constellation of corporate "sovereignties"—supersized legal "individuals" whose existence subverts the free market and threatens democracy and freedom (Backer 2007; Garrett 2008).

The Rise of Anti-Wal-Mart

Throughout the 1990s, Wal-Mart was generating over $10 billion in annual profits. Although previously distant from Washington, DC, Wal-Mart began to invest in political lobbying and campaign contributions, donating primarily to Republican candidates who were pro-business. By the year 2000, the company was using their growing political influence to shape the regulatory field to their advantage. They were fighting on many fronts, trying to ward off pro-union legislation, zoning ordinances, occupational health and safety standards, minimum wage increases, and healthcare legislation that would have required them to provide coverage to their associates. But by the mid-2000s, Wal-Mart was in trouble. Slower sales and rising costs lowered stock prices, and two of the company's biggest rivals—Target and Costco—were gaining strength (Bianco 2006, 266–267). To an extent, Wal-Mart was also suffering from its own success, even losing business to their own new stores.

Compounding the problem, the company had become, in the words of author Edward Humes, "a big, fat, and not particularly well-liked target, . . . a poster child for global warming, mass extinction, smog, and urban sprawl." Since its earliest years, the company had been ridiculed as low class and unsophisticated; kids who "got their clothes at Wal-Mart," for example, were fodder for schoolyard taunts. But opposition to Wal-Mart took on political dimensions as the company tried to enter communities who feared what a store would do to their local economy and landscape. Residents and city governments became protective of "mom and pop" stores, and worried about the eventual "killing" of their downtown areas. Opponents educated their neighbors about the downsides of "big-box" sprawl: traffic, litter, decreased property values, depressed wages, and environmental harm. Historical preservation groups joined communities to oppose the building of stores or supercenters on culturally significant sites. Some activists, like Sprawl-Busters [www.sprawl-busters.com/] founder Al Norman, even made stopping Wal-Mart and big box retail their profession.[4]

These reputational challenges were often exacerbated by the defensive, at times defiant, attitudes of the two CEOs—David Glass and Lee Scott—that succeeded Walton after his death in 1992. By 2004 the company was facing scores of scandals and lawsuits over labor abuses, unfair competition, and environmental damage. Adding to their headaches, in 2005, a leaked company memo [www.nytimes.com/packages/pdf/business/26walmart.pdf] revealed that nearly half of the children of Wal-Mart associates were either uninsured or receiving medical care through federal assistance programs [www.nytimes.com/2005/10/29/business/businessspecial2/29health.html?pagewanted=all].

Wal-Mart also has a fiercely oppositional relationship with the American labor movement. Unions and watchdog organizations see Wal-Mart as public enemy number one, and argue that the retailer has abused its power to lower wages and break unions across the retail and grocery sectors of the U.S. economy. Unions also oppose Wal-Mart's squeezing and outsourcing practices, claiming that they decrease employment opportunities in the U.S. and lead to questionable labor conditions in its primarily foreign supply chain. They have also raised public awareness about Wal-Mart's labor relations through collaborations with city governments as well as progressive media and watchdog websites—such as "Wal-Mart Watch" [http://makingchangeatwalmart.org/category/blog/]—that chronicle the company's policies and practices.

Moreover, controversies around the retailer routinely make their way into the national political arena. In 2000, Wal-Mart was hit with the largest class-action lawsuit in American history, *Dukes v. Walmart*, in which the plaintiffs accused the company of systematic gender discrimination in both hiring and promotion practices. The suit was originally filed by five former and current employees, but grew to include over 1.6 million women. The case called attention to the widespread under-representation of women in management, sizeable wage disparities among male and female managers, and embarrassing reports of sexism; the plaintiffs supported their claims with convincing and at times graphic details about the experiences of women across all positions within the company.

The mid-2000s were tough for Wal-Mart, capped by their inability to gain access to several major urban markets, including Los Angeles, New York, and Chicago. When the Los Angeles city council rejected supercenter in 2004, the company attempted to circumvent the municipal process by taking a ballot initiative straight to the people of neighboring Inglewood. Incensed by what many perceived as Wal-Mart's "lawless bullying," local residents organized furiously and voted against the company by a 60–40 margin. Wal-Mart, which had obsessively promoted itself as a symbol of America, was instead becoming a symbol of everything that had gone wrong with America. Acutely aware that no retailer in the U.S. had retained market dominance for more than one generation, Wal-Mart was determined to cheat fate (Humes 2011).

Fashioning the "Next Generation" Wal-Mart

Negative public perception presented a significant challenge just as the company was gearing up for intensive global and urban expansion. A survey conducted in 2004 indicated that between 2 and 8 percent of Wal-Mart shoppers had stopped patronizing the store because of bad publicity. After the embarrassment in Inglewood, Lee Scott established a semi-permanent "war room" with the goal of winning (back) the hearts and minds of consumers as well as politicians. They hired a public relations team that included former political strategists from both sides of the aisle, and they also began working with an environmental consultant (Meeks and Chen 2011; Humes 2011). One of the more prominent figures to be hired was Leslie Dach [http://investors.walmartstores.com/phoenix.zhtml?c=112761&p=irol-govBio&ID=47016], former Democratic presidential campaign advisor to John Kerry and member of both the Earth Defense Fund and the Audubon Society.

Wal-Mart believes that constructing a positive image in the twenty-first century requires "a set of strategic accommodations to its critics, especially . . . on environmental, racial, and cultural issues" (Lichtenstein 2009, 318), a metamorphosis that current CEO Mike Duke refers to as "The Next Generation Wal-Mart." These ongoing transformations are not simply responses to criticisms; rather, they are proactive attempts to appeal to an increasingly urban, liberal, multicultural, secular, and educated clientele—many of whom are skeptical of the company. At the same time, they also want to preserve their core business model, which relies on low wages and increased power and growth. These goals, which are sometimes at odds, have led to a host of strategies for depicting different aspects of Wal-Mart's business model as a free market solution to social problems, especially problems that were produced or exacerbated by those same markets, and Wal-Mart itself.

Though Wal-Mart had long presented itself as a champion for poor shoppers, these efforts took on new dimensions and intensity when they won praise from the African-American community for their heroic response to the victims of Hurricane Katrina in 2005. This mission was PR gold for Wal-Mart: not only was it a concrete example of the company providing relief to a poor African-American community in crisis, it positively showcased their massive size and efficiency. The sight of Wal-Mart delivery trucks distributing food and water to people effectively abandoned by the federal government would prove to be an indelible image of streamlined private enterprise success and governmental failure. Sensing a priceless photo-op, while workers were loading up their trucks with supplies, the company leaked footage of their preparations to conservative news outlets (Humes 2011, 98).

Building on the goodwill and momentum generated by their Katrina response, the company recently dedicated considerable resources to a corporate-wide sustainability initiative [www.walmartstores.com/Sustainability/7951.aspx]. The ambitious scope of their plans—as well as their progress thus far—have captured the imaginations of both the press and the public and have won over many former critics. This initiative represents the crown jewel of Wal-Mart's "next-generation" self-representation: by cultivating an image as an environmentally responsible company using its power to save the planet, Wal-Mart is ramping up its message that the free-market can "save the world" (Humes 2011).

This environmentalist turn began when then-CEO Lee Scott met with consultant Jib Ellison in 2004, at the nadir of the company's likeability and growth. According to journalist Edward Humes, Ellison convinced the skeptical but desperate executive that environmentalism—in deed as well as word—was a bona fide business opportunity that could lead to good publicity and measurable profits. Not only was the level of consumerism that Wal-Mart stores facilitated unsustainable, Ellison continued, but serious efforts toward going green would save Wal-Mart money. More importantly, by winning the hearts and minds of a new generation of environmentally-conscious consumers, it would contribute to the company's growth.

Scott set about developing a Sustainability Index that would place environmental impact ratings on all of Wal-Mart's products; the idea was to allow consumers to actively select greener products. Wal-Mart also announced three ambitious and long-term sustainability goals: 1) to be supplied by 100 percent renewable energy; 2) to create zero waste; and 3) to sell products that sustain our natural resources and environment. The Index and the Goals count on the company's ability to compel the supply chain to reduce waste and pollution. Wal-Mart now authors an annual Global Responsibility Report that measures its progress toward these goals,[5] and they now claim global leadership in environmentally sustainable sourcing. These efforts are part of a new attempt to rebrand the company as a responsible corporate citizen, and have likely played a role in lowering the number of Americans who view Wal-Mart in unfavorable terms, from 38 percent in 2005 to 20 percent in 2010 (Mitchell 2011).

The company points to a natural affinity between their legendary thrift and efficiency and the "reduce, reuse, recycle" ethos of sustainability programs. In 2010, current CEO Mike Duke [http://investors.walmartstores.com/phoenix. zhtml?c=112761&p=irol-govBio&ID=47019] and Leslie Dach outlined Wal-Mart's sustainability plans for the coming century: to reduce waste in the supply chain, to reduce global warming and deforestation, and to help meet the food needs of a growing population in developing countries.[6]

But to what extent can the same squeeze that forced so many vendors to cut environmental corners in their quest to reduce costs be retooled to enforce new environmental standards? Can saving the planet really be that easy? Environmentalists often dismiss insincere corporate public relations efforts as "greenwashing," but major organizations like the Sierra Club and Environmental Defense have applauded Wal-Mart's efforts, as have reports that Wal-Mart is "crushing" their sustainability goals (Sacks 2007). These standards have led former critics to partner with the company, including Adam Werbach (former president of the Sierra Club), who joined forces with Wal-Mart because of his frustration with environmentalists who were failing to frame their cause in terms that made sense to ordinary Americans.

Many former allies believe that people like Ellison and Werbach have lost their minds, sold their souls, or both. And there is good reason for such skepticism. While the new sustainability initiatives represent a significant improvement over Wal-Mart's prior production practices, the focus was—and always will be—"how [this] commitment would help Wal-Mart improve its bottom line" (Humes 2011, 78); any deviation from this goal would provoke a shareholder revolt. As a result, Wal-Mart's index necessarily normalizes unsustainable levels of environmental destruction. Even "green" Wal-Mart assumes that an economy fueled by rampant consumerism is natural and good, and that the aspirations of ordinary shoppers can be compatible with environmental protection.

Consider the strange juxtaposition at the 2011 Annual Shareholders' Meeting (ASM). Shortly before Leslie Dach extolled the virtues of the global sustainability initiative, C. Douglas McMillon [http://investors.walmartstores.com/phoenix.zhtml?c=112761&p=irol-govBio&ID=93428], President and CEO of Wal-Mart International, shared his unbridled enthusiasm for a cheap and colorful plastic plate that had already sold millions in Mexico. The goal of selling as many as possible seems fundamentally at odds with saving the planet. Similarly, the company's stated goal of having $1 billion of their grocery supply coming from "sustainable sources" by the year 2015 sounds impressive until we discover that Wal-Mart sold over $150 billion of groceries in 2010 in the U.S. alone. Signs also point to the company's willingness to celebrate shallower "harm reduction" efforts: in 2011 Shell Oil, a notorious polluter and abuser of human rights in Nigeria and elsewhere, was named "supplier of the year" for developing new packaging for motor oil.[7]

Journalist Jonathan Rowe (2011) warns that one danger of Wal-Mart's "greening" is that it diverts attention from the company's unsavory labor practices. Wal-Mart still primarily funds right-leaning politicians who oppose environmental protections and labor rights. According to Humes (2011), as Jib Ellison was convincing Lee Scott to replace the mindset of a low cost "race to the bottom" with a sustainable "race to the top," Ellison made connections to other issues:

"If you really want to take on sustainability with a capital 'S,' it's not just the environment. It's health care, it's wages, it's ethical sourcing, it's globalization. Everything. A sustainable society, a sustainable economy." Lee Scott replied, "Yes, but let's start with the environment."

(75)

These limits and ironies provide fodder for critics like journalist Stacy Mitchell, who writes for the environmentalist website grist [http://grist.org/], and who sees Wal-Mart's environmental epiphany as an opportunistic ploy to outflank criticisms of its size and the fundamental unsustainability of its business model. For Mitchell, Wal-Mart adapted not to change its core, but to continue it more effectively, and she points out that "some of the most serious environmental consequences of Wal-Mart's business model simply aren't on the table" (2012). She highlights the small changes in percentage points, the lack of progress on the Index, and the fact that it will take decades, even centuries, for Wal-Mart to meet its goals. Indeed, Wal-Mart's interest in environmentalism aims to perpetuate the commodified version of the American Dream as long as possible.

Anthropologists Peter Benson and Stuart Kirsh (2010) worry that we will stop thinking about the deeper changes needed in the consumer lifestyle and about "how industry is responsible for the current state of the environment" (474). Indeed, Wal-Mart's environmentalism neither questions its *right* to pollute, nor considers that rampant consumerism and big box retail might be *fundamentally* unsustainable. One potential ill effect of their sustainability campaign is to foster the dangerous illusion that the many serious environmental challenges the world faces can be resolved simply by choosing recycled products or sustainably sourced cotton. Can business and environmental bottom lines ever be reconciled? Can or should environmental sustainability be pursued as an independent variable, unconnected to human and labor rights? And if that is the model, exactly whose world is being saved, and at whose expense?

Wal-Mart Moving Forward

Indeed, many of the problems raised by critics will not be resolved without fundamental changes to the company, or to the legal environment that supports it. From Wal-Mart's perspective, the trick is to make changes that allow the company to have the strongest appeal to the widest range of shoppers. But what is at stake for the rest of us is not simply Wal-Mart's success or failure as a business, but what that success or failure means for *us*—the global public, the intended audience of this book.

In March 2012, *The New York Times* revealed [www.nytimes.com/2012/04/22/business/at-wal-mart-in-mexico-a-bribe-inquiry-silenced.html?pagewanted=all] that Wal-Mart executives in Mexico had bribed local officials in order to by-pass construction and zoning permits needed to build new stores. The bribes involved upwards of $24 million, and had taken place over a period of several years. It is also alleged that high-level Wal-Mart officials, including CEO Mike Duke, covered up the crimes (Barstow 2012). The scandal prompted several major pension funds to threaten divestiture from the company, two of who read shareholder proposals at the 2012 ASM. One called for greater transparency in the company's political contributions and specifically mentioned Wal-Mart's long-term relationship with the U.S. Chamber of Commerce, a group known to have lobbied for changes to the Foreign Corrupt Practices Act [www.justice.gov/criminal/fraud/fcpa/]—the law that Wal-Mart is alleged to have broken.

At the 2012 ASM, it was clear that Wal-Mart was shaken by these allegations. Rob Walton, Mike Duke, and C. Douglas McMillon promised that the company was cooperating with the federal investigation and that Wal-Mart would engage in the kind of "critical self-examination" that Sam would expect of them. Wal-Mart wants to present themselves as a benevolent company, but the bribery scandal disrupts this narrative. When benevolence is not possible, they strive for benign, and when benign is not believable, they try to be ordinary. When ordinary will not cut it, the company tries to be seen as inevitable. And when inevitability fails, the future of Wal-Mart is uncertain.

But this chapter argues that nothing is inevitable: not Wal-Mart, not the regulatory framework that facilitates its existence, and not the sociopolitical problems that the company purports to solve. Wal-Mart, like most human phenomena, is socially constructed, and its continued existence is contingent upon the same kinds of accidents, adaptation to circumstance, and degrees of popular legitimacy through which it emerged in the first place. By disassembling the behemoth that is Wal-Mart, we aim to demonstrate that the company can be not only de-constructed but transformed into something fundamentally different. The same is true for the ways we live, desire, and think.

The company's current vulnerability has the potential to re-animate Wal-Mart opponents who have grown discouraged by their seemingly unstoppable momentum. Wal-Mart's U.S. expansion plans may be complicated by the Mexico scandal: permits are getting scrutinized and city councils are revisiting land deals with the company (Clifford and Greenhouse 2012). Labor unions have linked the scandal squarely to the company's "growth at any cost" mentality. The stakes are high, as the battle over Wal-Mart is a battle over the American Dream itself.

3

WAL-MART NATION

Wal-Mart presents itself as unquestionably American: both an ordinary aspect of our landscape and a proudly patriotic institution. Wal-Mart believes that they are good for America and are a beacon of what makes our country great. Unashamed to wear its heart on its sleeve, it flies the stars and stripes in front of every store, and only recently altered its red, white, and blue color scheme.

Wal-Mart also offers a warm and enthusiastic welcome to customers from all backgrounds, ages, ethnicities, and income levels, and promotes a sense of community and mutual support among its employees and customers. Employees are portrayed as a "family" and shoppers are made to feel a part of "Wal-Mart Country." American society is projected as both harmonious and inclusive, as Wal-Mart is presented as a microcosm of the entire country.

Through this carefully crafted association with America, Wal-Mart employees and customers attain an experience of national belonging simply by shopping and working in the store. Shopping in Wal-Mart enables many of us to *feel* like Americans, because we are doing what ordinary Americans do, while working there promises a uniquely American version of economic and social mobility. Wal-Mart is a site where the American Dream becomes instantiated through consumer goods, welcoming inclusion, and patriotic displays. But aside from the fact that the company's founder and its first stores can be traced to northwest Arkansas, there is nothing inherently "American" about Wal-Mart; the association between the two is arbitrary. Wal-Mart's nationalist identity is actively defined and constructed through the beliefs, practices, and nationalist affect that circulate throughout the stores.

The Imagined Community

One of modern society's defining and most remarkable features is the fact that people experience *community*, defined as a sense of belonging together, with millions—often hundreds of millions—of people they have never met.

Benedict Anderson (1991) called this sense of belonging among strangers the imagined community of nationalism, and he described how it was made possible by the circulation of print media along capitalist trade routes. Anderson also suggests that what made nationalism so emotionally compelling was that, unlike in the monarchies of old, everyone was equal in their worth and belonging to the nation. For him, the magic of nationalism is the way that real differences between people—material matters of class, status, and power—disappear.

This chapter argues that one of the most impressive things about Wal-Mart is the way that they facilitate and actively promote a sense of belonging—both to the company and to the nation—among their employees and customers. We examine a range of ways that belonging is promoted through the use of visual icons like the company logo and the associates' blue vests, as well as through the philosophical education of their managers and the company's recent turn toward multiculturalism.

This powerful sense of belonging works synergistically with their patriotic image to help deflect criticisms and normalize Wal-Mart's presence on the social landscape, even among growing reports that the company, and the regulatory framework that enables it, is harming America. Cultivating a sense of belonging also helps smooth over the rough edges of being a Wal-Mart employee, and thus plays a significant preemptive role in their anti-union strategy.

Working for the Wal-Mart Family

Wal-Mart prides itself on a high degree of employee loyalty. Recognized as one of the retailer's core strengths, this loyalty is an effect of cultivating a sense of community: executives and managers know that employees who love and feel connected to the company are likely to steal less, work harder, and eschew labor unions—all of which translates into increased profits. Wal-Mart aims to shape and direct this sense of belonging in ways that are consistent with increasing its retail market share.

In Wal-Mart's early days, the company promoted itself as a cultural and political victory for Southern, rural, Christians—the residents of what historian Bethany Moreton calls the original "Wal-Mart Country" (2009). Moreton describes how Wal-Mart's management imported models of authority from Christian family life into the workplace. Nelson Lichtenstein (2009) also suggests that a strong emphasis on the heterosexual family and conservative values was probably reassuring to many of the company's earliest employees and especially appealing to rural Southern women who entered the workforce in droves after the 1950s (78). Wal-Mart's early efforts to promote a sense of family belonging benefited from the fact that their Ozark employees were fairly homogenous: most were poor, Christian, and white. Particularly in these years, Wal-Mart workers were a tightly-knit community and a source of mutual support.

Wal-Mart also fostered community through its store newsletter, *Wal-Mart World*, which celebrated the accomplishments of lower-tier employees (Moreton 2009, 104). Reading *Wal-Mart World* instilled in employees the feeling of belonging to a growing, yet still intimate, caring community. As the company grew beyond the Ozark region, the newsletter's reports of promotions, store events, and other tidbits, allowed workers to feel connected to other members of the larger Wal-Mart culture. *Wal-Mart World* has since moved into the digital age, and its content now appears under the heading "Associate Stories" [www.walmartstores.com/AboutUs/9447.aspx] under the corporate website's "Culture" banner.

Another way that Wal-Mart cultivated a loyal workforce was by hiring people who were marginalized by other industries—women, the elderly, and even the developmentally challenged. Take the case of Ben, someone we know well who worked at a Wal-Mart supercenter in north Texas for nearly five years in the 1990s. Ben had learning disabilities and a speech impediment and had always struggled, both in school and in social situations. Wal-Mart was his first and his longest running job. Working at Wal-Mart provided Ben with a positive identity: the work was meaningful, and he felt proud and productive. When asked during his tenure with the company about his goals in life, he answered sincerely that he hoped to "live and grow with Wal-Mart." It was easy to imagine that he would make sacrifices for the company. Ben worked hard, often arriving thirty minutes early in order to socialize. He became a checker and he dreamed of one day becoming an assistant manager. Ben's ultimate experience was disappointing—a story we will return to shortly—but his initial love for the company speaks volumes about the power of Wal-Mart's willingness to welcome and include their employees.

Imagining Camaraderie

Community is also promoted at Wal-Mart through a series of maneuvers specifically intended to obscure the hierarchy between workers and managers. This begins by replacing the word *employee* with *associate*, a move that invites both groups to imagine a partnership between equals, characterized by mutual benefit and individual respect. Moreover, instead of formal titles, Wal-Mart managers often encourage their hourly employees to address them by their first names, and to maintain joking or lighthearted relationships whenever possible. Such linguistic informality encourages team spirit to "bubble up" from those at the bottom (Walton 1992). Associates' equal membership in the community is also formalized through dress: their blue smocks, lanyards, and nametags impose uniformity and symbolize employees' membership in the company's culture.

Another strategy is the company's Open Door policy, begun by Sam himself, which purports to allow any associate with a grievance or suggestion the right to take their concern all the way to the CEO.[8] Though the policy borders on the unworkable—there are 1.4 million associates across the United States— Wal-Mart has retained it as one of the company's defining features. The company website explicitly links the Open Door policy to its family-oriented mentality: "We're all part of the same family—the Wal-Mart family. And like family, we care. The open door has helped solve some of our biggest problems, and it's generated some of our greatest ideas."[9] This rhetoric is substantiated by stories of Sam Walton listening to his employees that are legendary within the company. Indeed, a document now known as *Sam's Rules (for Building a Business)*, which is displayed both on store walls and in the Visitor Center (see Figure 3.1) lists both "appreciating" and "listening" as two of Walton's major tenets.

Figure 3.1 "Sam's Rules" pamphlet.

The sense of belonging to "the Wal-Mart Nation" is also reinforced through workplace rituals. At company picnics and annual shareholders' meetings, managers and executives often engage in mock rituals of inversion, where they are encouraged to allow their employees to embarrass and even humiliate them. Like the wordplay of the term associate, these inversion rituals break down the seriousness of the workplace, and trivialize official corporate hierarchies. Importantly, however, these rituals also reinforce the reality of workplace asymmetries, in that all associates continue to know their "place": the limited amount of power held by cashiers and shelf-stockers, for example, is made evident by the fact that they are the ones who are ritually allowed to usurp that power, if only for a few moments.

These symbolic inversions are interesting to anthropologists because they simultaneously disrupt and reinforce cultural hierarchies. Sam Walton was famous for engaging in these inversions. By helping out with low-level tasks, such as bagging groceries for a cashier or cutting meat in a supercenter deli, Walton demonstrated that the work itself was neither beneath him, nor anyone—a powerful message for the typically low status individuals in those positions. Such inversions were not accompanied, however, by material displacements: there was no ritual, where paychecks were swapped.

The best-known ritual engaged in by Wal-Mart associates—one which Walton adopted from a Korean company—is the morning cheer. The morning cheer cultivates community at many of the levels through which culture works: physical bodies joined in a ritualized chant, simultaneously reinforcing their sense of belonging, and building real feelings of team spirit:

Give me a W!—Give me an A!—Give me an L!
Give me a squiggly (employees shake their hips in unison)
Give me an M!—Give me an A!—Give me an R!—Give me a T!
What's that spell? Wal-Mart!
Whose Wal-Mart is it? It's my Wal-Mart!
Who's number one? The customer! Always!

By cheering for the company each morning, Wal-Mart employees remind one another that they are united by a common purpose. Walton understood that community—like culture—needed to be performed, both with daily habits and from the ground up.

The Annual Shareholders' Meeting

The company's efforts to cultivate an "imagined Wal-Mart community" are displayed most visibly at the Annual Shareholders' Meeting (ASM) and company

Figure 3.2 Associates at company picnic during the 2011 ASM.

picnic, held in June on the University of Arkansas campus in Fayetteville. At least five thousand associates, from every country where the company has stores, are flown in, housed, fed, and entertained (see Figure 3.2). For four days, they are treated to a mix of live music, free food and gifts, and various tours, including of the company's headquarters, downtown Bentonville, and the Wal-Mart Visitor Center. All this activity culminates with the actual meeting in the Bud Walton Arena. One associate from every other store is chosen to attend; they are elected by their peers, and must "run" on platforms of enthusiasm, experience and company pride. Attendees wear colorful country-coded t-shirts and Wal-Mart pins and memorabilia to showcase their pride and spirit (see Figure 3.3): the more pins and buttons attached to one's lanyard, for example, the more "connected" an employee seems to the company and its belief system.

During the ASM, Wal-Mart's international associates descend upon Benton-ville's town square in waves. Because many do not speak English and are inexperienced travelers, they stay safely clustered with their Wal-Mart peers, moving around the square in a series of seemingly choreographed steps: posing for photographs in front of the town's Confederate statue; circulating through

Figure 3.3 Canadian associates peering into the window of the original Five and Dime.

and endlessly photographing the Visitor Center; pausing in the coffee shop where, in 2011, many enthusiastically submitted to temporary tattoos of Sam's Ford pickup truck and the Wal-Mart "spark" (see Figure 3.4); and then piling back onto their respective buses to be taken to their Fayetteville lodgings. In the afternoon that we spent observing and talking with the 2011 arrivals, we saw the Chilean and Puerto Rican groups pose and perform the Wal-Mart cheer in front of their respective flags, and the United Kingdom group break into a custom-lyricized version of the Depeche Mode hit "I Just Can't Get Enough" (of Wal-Mart's low prices).

Christian Capitalism and Servant Leadership

As Wal-Mart expanded in the 1980s, the company recruited a primarily male managerial force from small, conservative, and less academically competitive colleges across the American South. Many of these men were former members of Students in Free Enterprise (SIFE) [www.sife.org/Pages/default.aspx], an organization whose goals are to foster and publicize the connections between Christianity, capitalism, and entrepreneurship (Lichtenstein 2009; Moreton

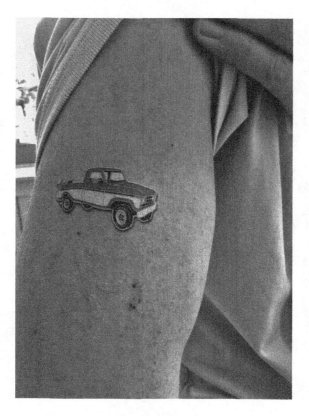

Figure 3.4 Wal-Mart associates give themselves temporary tattoos at the 2011 ASM.

2009). Wal-Mart soon became the largest benefactor of SIFE, awarding a number of "free enterprise fellowships" and encouraging both company executives and vendors to serve as program advisors and financial backers. SIFE is one of many corporate-academic amalgamations that support free-market minded groups on a growing number of campuses.

Central to SIFE's philosophy is the concept of "servant leadership," an ideology that frames the ideal role of managers as servants of their employees and customers. Included as one of nine elements of Wal-Mart's culture [www. walmartstores.com/AboutUs/295.aspx], servant leadership is both a doctrine and a management style that prioritizes caring and service between all employees—regardless of rank or seniority—as well as between employees and customers. For Moreton, this kind of thinking, "explained away the discrepancy between low wages and high employee loyalty" with relative success (2009, 108). In 1985, Sam and Helen Walton established the Walton International Scholars Program, in order to spread the free enterprise message to an increasingly Protestant Central America. A Nicaraguan participant in the program, interviewed by conservative radio host Paul Harvey, stated: "I met Sam Walton twice in person and quickly came to learn that financial success and Christianity were perfectly compatible: being successful and humble, being loving and demanding, being competitive and caring for others—all of these were compatible" (Moreton 2009, 223).

Whether or not these beliefs are compatible, it is clear that servant leadership helps Wal-Mart elaborate a plausible worldview in which the activities of the company, which are often described as cutthroat, are seen as consistent with Christian values. This is a significant way that Wal-Mart cultivates a management team who shares its core values, and encourages hourly employees to take pride in being part of a mission that makes low prices available to customers.

The Limits of Community

Although Wal-Mart effectively deploys their company spirit, their efforts to promote community often run into conflict with their overriding commitment to profit. In addition to voicing concern about meager wages, Wal-Mart associates express frustration with heavy workloads, unpredictable (and at times retaliatory) scheduling, unaffordable benefits, and slim prospects for advancement.

Additional divisions exist along the lines of race, gender, religion, and sexual orientation. Concerns about disparities and discrimination, which are commonly expressed, undermine the sense of horizontal comradeship within the organization, and can lead to lawsuits (see Chapter 4). Frustration with management can compel some employees to quit (Wal-Mart has one of the highest turnover rates in the industry), to steal from the company, or to try to form a union (see Chapter 5). In fact, several community-building rituals, the term "associates," and Wal-Mart's profit-sharing program were implemented in response to unionization efforts in the early 1970s. Wal-Mart's frequent failure to achieve a stable sense of belonging within their company is, of course, not unique; it is symptomatic of many of the ways that America routinely fails to include its entire citizenry in national political and economic life. The failure is compounded at Wal-Mart, however, by their corporate culture and management practices.

Wal-Mart's practices around employee termination evince yet another gap in the company's orchestrated Christian family image. In order to pay less unemployment insurance, Wal-Mart strives to keep its terminations low and its resignations high. Unsatisfactory employees are often "encouraged" to quit with inconvenient shifts, last-minute schedule changes, or reduced hours. At times, however, the company will fire employees they see as problems, and they have no patience for worker theft. Being terminated by Wal-Mart serves as a very rude awakening for loyal employees, some of whom are let go for mistakes that others might view as honest or forgivable, a situation that can lead to feelings of betrayal by the company they have served with pride. This was the case with our friend Ben, who, when we left him, had worked his way up to a cashier position. One busy day, a single mother shopping with her children came through Ben's line. She pleaded with Ben to give her baby formula for free, saying she could not afford it. Ben was torn. He looked at her children, her sad eyes, and his long checkout line. In a decision he would forever regret, he gave her the formula.

When Wal-Mart management found out, they accused Ben of theft and fired him on the spot; he was told to leave and was banned from the store. For Ben, this experience was a shattering one; his entire world had fallen apart and he went home feeling crushed. Ben returned to the store the following week to apologize and ask for his job back, but a manager threatened to call security. A few weeks later, Ben's devoutly Christian grandmother, after witnessing the pain of Ben's disgrace, called the store manager to ask for a second chance. No match for her persuasive kindness, the manager relented, but by then Ben was too embarrassed and did not want to return to the store as a "thief."

A year later, Ben moved with his family to a smaller north Texas town where he applied at the local Wal-Mart, only to discover that he had been placed on a "do not hire" list. Ben's choices for work—in a small town with few skills— were severely limited, and his hopes dwindled as he considered his remaining options—primarily fast food restaurants. Years later, Ben still feels betrayed, especially given how much he loved the company and how hard he had worked for them, and he resents the way that he was shunned by the Wal-Mart family.

Wal-Mart and Multiculturalism

The constructed nature of Wal-Mart's nationalist identity becomes especially apparent in its attempts to appeal to a multicultural market. Multiculturalism presumes the equal validity and worth of all cultural traditions and the belief that diversity is both a reality and a source of strength. An important tenet of this philosophy is that the recognition of one cultural tradition need not hurt or minimize the value of any other: theoretically, all can peacefully co-exist. For the service industry, particularly retail, multiculturalism makes good business sense, in that it promises to increase the number of customers who feel "at home" in the store. For Wal-Mart, this has translated into a series of transformations—some larger and more permanent than others—that cater to different "cultural" groups: Latinos, Asians, African-Americans, gays and lesbians, college students, and even "upscale" consumers toward whom the company has increased its marketing. These transformations do not funda- mentally disrupt the overall white, Christian, and heterosexual identity with which the company continues to strongly identify, but they do begin to widen the scope of who is included in "the Wal-Mart Nation."

Wal-Mart's multiculturalism is evident in stores located near large minority and immigrant communities in the United States. An excellent example is the Supercenter in Springdale, Arkansas, which makes specific efforts to target the Latino clientele. Springdale [www.springdaleark.org/] is a fairly small town of just under 70,000 people. It is a short drive from Bentonville, and is home to Tyson chicken. Since the 1990s, when the passage of the North American Free Trade Act (NAFTA) [http://topics.nytimes.com/topics/reference/timestopics/subjects/n/north_american_free_trade_agreement/index.html] displaced tens of thousands of Mexican agricultural workers, Springdale has seen its Latino immigrant population boom. Latinos now make up 20 percent of the town, with many working in Tyson processing plants, a demographic change noticeable with the number of *panaderias* and *taquerias* that dot the landscape. Wal-Mart's multicultural efforts will undoubtedly increase given recent census data predicting that whites will no longer be an ethnic majority in the United States by the year 2050.

Most of the section signs in the Springdale store are in Spanish, visible in slightly smaller print below the English. The walls contain large photographic images of non-white people, presumably meant to represent the multicultural clientele. The models are not explicitly coded as "Latino," yet the photographs are clearly designed to make non-white and female shoppers feel "at home" in the store. These visual efforts are augmented by the product selection. In addition to aisles marked as containing "Hispanic" foods, the store features specific cuts of meat, and several other products targeting Latino consumers on a series of endcaps: hundred-count packages of tortillas are available, not only from established and local brands, but also from Wal-Mart's far cheaper house brand; greeting cards and custom cakes are available for *quinceaneras* and other Latino holidays and events; and the produce section stocks a wide variety of chili peppers and other vegetables used in Mexican and Latino cuisine.

Wal-Mart's efforts toward a more "diverse" Supercenter are ripe for anthropological inquiry: Do their efforts entice more Latinos into the store? Is the "cultural" identity of these shoppers enhanced, diminished, or altered through their experience with Wal-Mart? What types of cultural diversity or intercultural exchange are made possible—*and impossible*—by Wal-Mart's entry into multicultural retail?

An excellent starting point for such an investigation would be to compare the store to a local Latino competitor (see Figure 3.5). Just a few minutes' drive from the supercenter, *Mi Tienda* (My Shop) offers Latino shoppers everything that Wal-Mart does not: a full Mexican *carniceria*, filled with regional

Figure 3.5 Produce section at *Mi Tienda*, Springdale, Arkansas.

delicacies, most of which cannot be found at Wal-Mart. Each aisle contains signature products from nearly every major region of Mexico and Central America, placed there by an owner who wants to enable connections between his customers and their "home" countries. The store also houses a lunch counter specializing in delicious Mexican street food. Frequently, *Mi Tienda* doubles as a center for the Latino immigrant community and often provides space in their parking lot for community members to stage cultural and religious events. On a Saturday afternoon in December, we watched dozens of school-age students perform an Aztec-inflected dance honoring the Virgin of Guadalupe, Mexico's patron saint, while enjoying steaming cups of *chocolate*, homemade *tamales* and decadent Mexican sweets—all prepared and distributed for free by community members, including *Mi Tienda's* staff.

The owners of *Mi Tienda* are not worried about competition from Wal-Mart, who they see as "good neighbors." But they may face a serious challenge from Wal-Mart's multicultural push. If many of their customers buy their basic goods—beans, milk, bread, tortillas, vegetables, certain cheeses, meats, and even their holiday cakes—more cheaply from Wal-Mart, and only use *Mi Tienda* for more "authentic" or hard to find items, the store may struggle to remain

Figure 3.6 Dancers celebrating the feast of the Virgin of Guadalupe in the *Mi Tienda* parking lot, December 2010.

in business. Underpaid immigrant workers may prefer *Mi Tienda* but may not be able to resist Wal-Mart's low prices. Ominously, the owners of *Mi Tienda* told us that they had to ask two Wal-Mart marketing representatives, who were photographing entire shelves of products for future study, to please stop.

Wal-Mart stocks their shelves with many of the same brands as those carried by *Mi Tienda*. But by excluding low-volume items, or those that may not appeal to white shoppers, Wal-Mart's multicultural offerings leave out many meaningful items, along with their unique tastes, smells, memories, and associations. These are integral parts of culture that could be diminished were *Mi Tienda* to succumb to Wal-Mart's retail dominance. If Wal-Mart's embrace of multiculturalism puts stores like *Mi Tienda* out of business, it would actually reduce diversity; first, by removing a store that is also a center of Latino community, and second by reducing the aesthetic and "everyday" experience of being Latino in Springdale.

A final consideration regarding Wal-Mart's multicultural efforts concerns the way that its symbolic inclusion of other cultures in dominant spaces can obscure the ways that these same groups are legally and physically excluded from the nation, treated as criminals, dehumanized through phrases like "illegal," regarded as second-class citizens, and deported. Wal-Mart's multicultural policies may make non-citizen shoppers feel included as customers, and may reassure white shoppers that they live in an inclusive society, but they may also render invisible forms of anti-immigrant violence and structural inequality that confront these "multicultural" communities.

A Patriotic Company?

Wal-Mart has actively promoted its symbolic connection to the "country" at large, and an image of itself as patriotic. This was how the company publicized its quick disaster response in New Orleans following Hurricane Katrina. In another example, the Wal-Mart Military Family Promise program [www.walmartstores.com/pressroom/news/10582.aspx] guarantees a job of equal salary to the family members of military personnel forced to move because of their spouse's service. They also gave $1.1 million in Christmas toys and books for the children of military families, and laid 16,000 wreaths at national cemeteries.[10] But many of Wal-Mart's corporate practices provoke questions about the depth of its patriotism, particularly regarding their super low wages and their outsourcing of American jobs.

In reaction to groups who present their private economic interests as "national" concerns, some critics promote an alternative vision of patriotism. The Rebuild the Dream [http://rebuildthedream.com/splash-v3/] movement is one example.[11] Environmental activist Van Jones [http://vanjones.net/], the former "Green Jobs" czar for the Obama Administration and the President and co-founder of Rebuild the Dream, draws a contrast between "Deep Patriots" and "Cheap Patriots." He thinks this distinction adds "clarification and moral nuance" to the Occupy Wall Street Movement [http://occupywallst.org/about/], whose rhetoric relies on a division between "the 99 percent" and "the 1 percent" (Jones 2012). Instead, he suggests that "Americans admire success. What we detest is greed. We like economic winners; we hate economic cheaters. We cheer economic innovation; we despise financial manipulation." He also argues that:

[W]e expect everyone in America—the 100 percent—to do their best, to be good neighbors and to contribute to the success of our country.

In return for enjoying the support of the greatest nation on earth, we expect those who do well *in* America to do well *by* America. We expect them to pay fair taxes, create good jobs here at home, to give something back to this country.

These criticisms, which call for a good faith commitment to restoring and creating economic fairness, mirror specific criticisms of Wal-Mart made by unions and many Wal-Mart associates.

Conclusion

Wal-Mart provides an excellent example of how organizations work to promote a sense of belonging and channel it for their own purposes. Central to this practice is the erasure of differences in rank and value between individuals. The obstacles Wal-Mart encounters in its attempt to graft a harmonious community, rooted in equality, onto a capitalist logic of corporate profit, as well as the alternative understandings that place a sense of belonging and mutual obligation prior to the bottom line (and that recognize the tension between these ideals), illuminate different conceptions of belonging in American society.

4

THE PEOPLE
OF WAL-MART

In March 2011, The Wal-Mart Foundation donated $2 million dollars and six thousand items of business-wear to Dress for Success (DFS) [www.dressfor success.org/], a New York City-based organization whose mission is to assist low-income women prepare for the workplace. Wal-Mart's press release, which emphasized the "desperate"[12] need of DFS's clients, as well as Wal-Mart's commitment to working women, was distributed widely; it was soon followed by a video, which was uploaded to the "Community Journal" page of Wal-Martnyc.com, the company website (now known as nyc.walmartcommunity.com [http://nyc.walmartcommunity.com/]) dedicated to "separating the facts from the fiction"[13] about Wal-Mart's mostly unsuccessful attempts to establish stores in New York City. In addition to interviews with Joi Gordon, CEO of Dress for Success, and Mary Fox, Wal-Mart's Senior Vice President of Global Apparel Sourcing, the video prominently features one of the collaboration's greatest success stories—Lyneese Roldan. A stylish African-American woman in her early thirties who, according to Ms. Gordon, was "homeless" and "living couch-to-couch" prior to working with DFS, Lyneese is presented as living proof of the attainability of the American Dream for women of color willing to make the personal changes necessary for success. Through a DFS program called the *Going Places Network*, Ms. Roldan secured steady employment with cosmetics icon Bobbi Brown. For Lyneese, "[i]t was the greatest day of [her] life," and she tells the viewer, in no uncertain terms: "I am going places. And I know this. So I'm very grateful."[14]

The *Going Places Network*, a 12-week skills enhancement course sponsored by Wal-Mart, is an extension of a pilot program that the company launched with DFS in 2009 "in response to [the country's] challenging economic climate."[15] According to DFS's website, the Network is intended to "help unemployed and under-employed Dress for Success clients gain professional skills, accelerate their job search and build confidence through weekly train-ing sessions, one-on-one career coaching and networking in a supportive environment."[16] The pilot program was deemed successful enough for Wal-Mart to make their $2 million donation, enabling DFS to expand the program to 60 U.S. cities.

One of the earliest cities to receive a substantial sum of the money was Chicago. Though the city has very recently begun to open its borders to Wal-Mart, Chicago was slow to embrace the retail giant, due to the same kinds of concerns expressed by New Yorkers (Jones 2010). Wal-Mart used DFS to smooth their passage into both these cities through the bodies of these women, specifically their public displays of mobility and gratitude. By wearing suits manufactured for Wal-Mart, and by having their job training linked to the company's patronage, participants in the *Going Places Network* were repackaged as affective stakeholders in Wal-Mart's success. This philanthropy reinforced Wal-Mart's carefully cultivated self-image as a path to economic independence for impoverished, non-white women.

Less than two weeks after this media flurry, the United States Supreme Court heard opening arguments for a lawsuit known as *Wal-Mart v. Dukes* [www.supremecourt.gov/opinions/10pdf/10–277.pdf]. Betty Dukes, the plaintiff, was then a 60-year-old African-American woman from California. Dukes has worked for Wal-Mart since 1994, and in 2001, along with four other former and current employees, she filed a sex discrimination suit that claimed she had been denied the training and opportunity she needed to advance within the company. The suit further alleged that "Wal-Mart discriminates against its female employees in making promotions, job assignments, pay decisions and training, and retaliates against women who complain against such practices."[17] After Ms. Dukes' initial filing, 1.6 million additional women signed on, representing a substantial portion of the women who have worked for Wal-Mart since the cutoff date of December 26, 1998.

One key issue in the case was whether the women could sue the company as a "class"—that is, as a group of people who had been collectively injured by the same individual or organization. In order to be considered a class, the plaintiffs' attorneys had to demonstrate that Wal-Mart treated women *as a whole* differently than they did men—an allegation upheld by a previous court, which had found "significant proof of a corporate policy of discrimination" (Rushe 2011). Not surprisingly, Wal-Mart vehemently disputed these allegations, and appealed the case all the way to the Supreme Court. Not only did Wal-Mart vigorously deny the charges of discrimination, they also insisted that their 4,000-plus stores are too different from one another—in size, location, workforce, and overall character—for the company to be guilty of the systematic behavior alleged by the plaintiffs.

In June 2011, The Supreme Court ruled against Betty Dukes and her peers, having decided that the plaintiffs had "little in common but their sex and their lawsuit."[18] Though individual women are still free to sue the company of their own accord, the justices were unanimous that they could no longer proceed as a class. The Court was divided, however, about whether the company had engaged in widespread discrimination, and all three female justices (in addition to Justice Breyer) dissented from the majority opinion on that point. The decision was a clear financial and ideological victory for Wal-Mart. A successful class-action lawsuit could have not only cost the company billions of dollars, but might also have set a precedent affecting core elements of their business model, a model that relies heavily on the routine and systematic subordination of certain groups of people.

*   *   *

This chapter explores the question of how Wal-Mart maintains its legitimacy by critically examining competing claims—advanced by the company and its critics—about the "people of Wal-Mart." One of the most important sources of Wal-Mart's legitimacy is its democratic openness to poor shoppers from all social groups, an implicit promise to make the American Dream accessible to all. This openness has earned Wal-Mart criticism from those who believe themselves superior to the people at Wal-Mart, an elitism that strengthens the company's populist image. Furthermore, Wal-Mart presents itself as a ladder to success for its associates, many of whom come from disadvantaged backgrounds. Wal-Mart expresses eternal gratitude to their associates, and presents the opportunities they offer as a cancellation of their debt.

However, there is a wide gulf between Wal-Mart's self-image and the experience of many employees for whom Wal-Mart is a low paying and "dead end" job. These negative experiences reinforce a host of criticisms from progressive groups who allege that Wal-Mart intentionally discriminates against female and non-white employees, and others who contend that their business model relies on a low wage workforce that is disproportionately female and minority. This model, some contend, depresses wages throughout the economy, and cultivates a captive customer base who cannot afford to shop elsewhere. In response to these critiques, which complicate their efforts to expand into urban markets, Wal-Mart has engaged in a host of PR and philanthropic activities in order to more aggressively promote itself as a harmonious multicultural company interested in promoting the well-being of non-whites and women.

These representations obscure the company's chronic exploitation of structural inequalities; they also render the history and depth of these problems —along with more holistic, long term, and collective solutions to them— invisible. Wal-Mart's focus on individual market discipline as a solution for social inequality leaves these problems both unresolved and "normal." The

question of whether or not Wal-Mart is "good for women" or other disadvantaged groups thus reveals tensions between group and individual
identities. While Wal-Mart's solution might work for individual women, it comes
at the expense of a collective that is left behind. Finally, the strategy of the
Dukes case, while critical of Wal-Mart, reinforces the individual, market-based
model of social advancement that acts as a horizon of possibility in the dominant
political imaginary.

People of Wal-Mart

One truly democratic aspect of Wal-Mart is that virtually everyone is welcome
as a customer. Wal-Mart's business model focused on poor, rural, white
communities in its early years, and they continue to target poor, nonwhite,
and urban customers. Wal-Mart also hires entry-level employees from all walks
of life, many without college degrees. Approximately 57 percent of Wal-Mart's
workforce is female, and the company is also one of America's largest private
employers of racial minorities.[19]

Some Americans think that the door at Wal-Mart is open too wide. Consider
the popular website (and book) People of Wal-Mart [www.peopleofwalmart.
com/] (Kipple et al. 2010),[20] an expanding library of images, taken from
Wal-Mart stores, of customers and employees who appear to be poor, rural,
overweight, gay, lesbian, transgendered, unfashionable, costumed, or just plain
bizarre. People of Wal-Mart encourages visitors to laugh at and judge a group
of individuals depicted as ridiculous and pathetic. Although the individuals
are of different ages and ethnicities, most "targets" share a low socioeconomic
class.

Such criticisms only reinforce Wal-Mart's image as a champion for ordinary
people. Wal-Mart's embrace of the poor and unsophisticated, however,
while more inclusive than People of Wal-Mart, still reinforces a notion of social
ranking. The company encourages "disadvantaged" people to engage in self-
improvement and class mobility through aspirational consumption and savings.
While some may see this as contrived, detractors often neglect the concrete
ways that Wal-Mart *is* improving the quality of many people's lives. "Save
Money, Live Better" is not just a slogan, it is an experience shared by many
shoppers. People *feel* things about Wal-Mart: loyal customers and employees
repeatedly narrate not only a sense of belonging but also of accomplishment
and efficiency in making financially-savvy enhancements to their daily routines.
Through convenient locations, fully-stocked shelves, extended hours, lay-away
plans, and reliable EDLP, Wal-Mart stores become places where shoppers of
limited means can dream: of more Christmas presents under the tree, of a
more elaborate welcome home party for a returning soldier, or of a meal with

restaurant-quality ingredients for a family with limited disposable income. Indeed, many of the company's most vocal proponents are attentive consumers who understand themselves in the upwardly mobile terms of the American Dream.

Mom-preneurs

Wal-Mart's practice of addressing their customers as individuals actively engaged in self-improvement through practical consumption is also evident with the "Wal-Mart Moms" [http://instoresnow.walmart.com/Community.aspx] featured on the company's website.[21] This group was named by pollsters after they were identified in the 2004 presidential campaign as a key swing-voter group that leaned toward George W. Bush. Wal-Mart seized the opportunity to turn these women into a market demographic, conducting a great deal of research on their consumer preferences and habits, as well as their broader political and social outlook, and expressive repertoire. One way they have done this is by cultivating relationships with web-savvy moms who blog and tweet about the relationships between shopping and their everyday lives. This has included sponsored trips to Bentonville where moms sampled new products, met with the actor Harrison Ford, and networked with Wal-Mart-sponsored business connections (Neff 2008).

The women claim authenticity: "We're real Moms. And we're bloggers. We've come together with Wal-Mart to celebrate Moms, share our experiences and create a community." According to their introductory group post, "We've been asked by Wal-Mart to simply represent the voice of all moms."[22] The discussion topics are "lifestyle" focused, and include parenting, "green living," health, and politics. The "Moms on Politics" section reminds female consumers of their swing-voter significance and encourages their participation in upcoming elections. Wal-Mart is intensely interested in the unvarnished opinions of these women on a range of topics, as well as in convincing the public of their collective consumer wisdom.

For Wal-Mart, the blogs provide a wealth of information about women's shopping preferences, and enable Wal-Mart to further disseminate its brand of family-oriented, everyday, and practical provisioning. The site invites low- and middle-income women who surf it to see themselves as part of a broader community of "Wal-Mart moms" who face similar problems and concerns. The "mompreneurs," as they are cheerfully described on the company's website, epitomize the consumer-oriented version of the American Dream that Wal-Mart seeks to promote, and portray the company as a trusted partner in self-improvement. While the site appeals to "all moms," these blogs do *not* invite female readers to understand themselves in the terms of the 1.6 million women that sued Wal-Mart, i.e., as part of a collective subject seeking equality, though it is certain that a sizeable number of Wal-Mart's female consumers have experienced gender-based discrimination in their own lives.

Climbing the Wal-Mart Ladder

In the U.S., social hierarchy is typically understood through the metaphor of the ladder to success, and many of us view the climb as integral to achieving the Dream. Through faith in the existence of equal opportunity—often referred to as one's "shot" at the top—many Americans believe that effort determines rank, and that individuals choose their social position, regardless of background. In this imaginary, disciplinary self-fashioning becomes the ideal site and measure of citizenship. One downside in keeping with this narrative is that it leads many of us to turn to beliefs about the qualities and capabilities of "women and minorities" in order to explain their so-called failure to climb the ladder.

The most explicit way that Wal-Mart markets its vision of social mobility is by promoting the legend of Sam Walton, whose life the company narrates as one of hard work, tenacity, and the ultimate attainment of the American Dream. This carefully constructed biography studiously avoids the elements of his success that were not the result of individual effort. By relegating these factors to the background, Wal-Mart's official "story" of social mobility is substantiated—even glorified—while the more complex one of pervasive social inequality remains untold. Indeed, Sam Walton is presented as a role model for everyone, especially Wal-Mart associates, regardless of his or her race, class, or gender.

Wal-Mart's commercial advertising aggressively promotes this vision, using members of minority groups to foreground the opportunities for social mobility offered by the company. In television, internet, and print promotions, Wal-Mart celebrates its ability and willingness to create good, meaningful jobs, particularly those that advance the careers of women and minority groups. A typical television spot [www.youtube.com/watch?v=BDv5-LDQeus] features Tejas, a recent Indian immigrant who works as a customer service manager in Idaho. As we watch the smiling Tejas interact with various customers, the shift manager's voice tells us that Tejas has been named "associate of the month" more than once, due to the ways that he "exemplifies respect for the individual." The manager tells us that Tejas was promoted into management after only six months, while yet another voice adds: "He looks at his job as if it is a privilege to be here, which makes it a privilege for us to work with him." For his part, Tejas only reinforces this message of mobility: "There is definitely 100 percent opportunity [here]. If you work, you will get rewarded. As everybody knows, America is the land of opportunity."

Another commercial [www.youtube.com/watch?v=_XerYWlS_tA] features an associate named Noemi, a middle-aged Latina from Texas who tells the viewer that she raised her sons on welfare during the 1980s. However, Noemi says that "After [she] got the job at Wal-Mart, things started changing." She explains: "I wrote a letter to the food stamp office, [saying] 'Thank you very much, I don't need you anymore.'" In this ad, receiving resources through governmental redistribution is presented as a reason for shame, a sign of personal failure and dependency. Visibly choking up, Noemi continues: "You know, now I can actually say I bought my home. I know that the more I dedicated, the harder I worked, this is going to benefit my family." As Noemi speaks, we see a picture of her alongside Sam Walton. The commercial posts a statistic claiming that "73 percent of Wal-Mart's store management team started as hourly associates," but does not reveal the percentage of hourly associates that "make it" into management (the substance of *Wal-Mart v. Dukes* and a figure that the company does not make available). At the end of the commercial, Noemi introduces her son, Mario, who also works at Wal-Mart; she beams: "I believe Mario is following in my footsteps."

Though we are meant to feel as if we "know" something about Noemi through this intimate portrait, we are not privy to the details of Noemi's life that allowed her to say "No thank you" to the government assistance that helped her raise her children. As with the edited version of Sam's biography, the elements of Noemi's "success story" that are not derived from her relationship with capitalist free enterprise are downplayed, if not erased entirely. This narrative is misleading and very important to disrupt. Though Wal-Mart claims to have freed Noemi from her dependence on food stamps, there is ample evidence that many of the company's employees require government assistance—specifically food stamps—in order to make ends meet (Dube and Jacobs 2004a; Wal-Mart Watch 2008; Miles 2012). Furthermore, by taking sole credit for assisting Noemi, Wal-Mart trivializes the fact that this woman successfully raised a family with help from a meager federal assistance wage. Wal-Mart's representation also presents Noemi's capacity to "work hard" solely in terms of her labor for the company, and omits what she *has already accomplished* on behalf of her two sons, one of whom now "follow[s] in [her] footsteps." Though government assistance had long helped to stabilize Noemi's life, Wal-Mart's re-packaging of her story treats such assistance as an impediment—rather than a facilitator—of social mobility and financial independence.

These commercials encourage us to celebrate the small number of Wal-Mart employees who "make it," and to ignore the great majority who are routinely passed over. Wal-Mart's success stories are carefully selected to emphasize the company's "truth": that individual hard work is the only path to upward mobility and full (consumer) citizenship. Furthermore, in a powerful sense, this opportunity at social mobility is presented as canceling the debt that Wal-Mart owes to their associates.

Complicating Wal-Mart's Mobility Narrative

Missing from Wal-Mart's inclusion narrative are the structural realities and historical processes through which certain groups became disadvantaged. For African-Americans, for example, this includes the slave trade, lynching, segregation, restrictive zoning, gentrification, predatory lending, the war on drugs, and negative media representations; for women the list might include a gendered division of labor, sexual assault and rape, objectification, and their systematic exclusion from positions of authority. Furthermore, both women and racial minorities have been, in the aggregate and individually, uniquely disadvantaged by neoliberal economic policies that have decreased public spending and social protections. In addition, Wal-Mart's definition of social exclusion, and the individualized, market based solutions they recommend, ignore the forms of collective social and political agency, such as labor unions and the progressive movements of the 1960s and 70s, that sought to address the structural roots of inequality. These groups and their many contemporary manifestations, like Occupy Wall Street and Rebuild the Dream, focus on leveling the playing field and promoting more access to material resources for marginalized populations. In this way, Wal-Mart's representational strategy reproduces a central tenet of neoliberal thought, that of rendering progressive movements irrelevant, and proposing market mechanisms as the sole means to resolving social inequality.

Also absent in this characterization is the role that Wal-Mart's business model plays in constructing and maintaining these inequalities. Numerous critics highlight the disparity between Wal-Mart's promise of social mobility and the reality of its "dead end" jobs. Wal-Mart, for its part, takes no responsibility for low wages, insisting that: "retail and service wages *are what they are*" (Quinn 2005, 6; our emphasis). This narrative normalizes Wal-Mart's pay structure and treats wages as a free-floating fact, unaffected by the company's business model and the neoliberal regulatory framework as a whole. It also ignores numerous lawsuits that implicate Wal-Mart in wage violations and outright wage theft, and the fact that Wal-Mart's associates are some of the lowest paid employees in the United States. Sales associates currently average $8.81 per hour (Moberg 2011), and a recent study concludes that Wal-Mart pays average wages significantly lower than any other retail or big box (Jacobs et al. 2011). These rates are compounded by the company's history of pushing experienced (and better paid) employees out [www.nytimes.com/2005/10/26/business/26 walmart.ready.html?pagewanted=all] in order to reduce labor costs.

Nelson Lichtenstein likens Wal-Mart's pay and promotion structure to "a short stack of pancakes with a long thin strawberry perched in the middle" (2009, 128). And while corporate attention is focused on the strawberries— individuals like Tejas and Noemi—stories of "the rest," i.e., the millions of disaffected, betrayed, injured, exhausted, and still-struggling employees for whom Wal-Mart's promise remains unrealized, crowd the internet on sites like Working at WAL-MART [http://workingatwal-mart.blogspot.com/] and Wal-MartSucks.org [http://walmartsucksorg.blogspot.com/].[23] For the majority, advancement is arduous and elusive.

As with other putatively meritocratic organizations, promotions at Wal-Mart are based on allegedly neutral standards related to experience, training, and personal characteristics, such as leadership skills and decision-making ability. Normalizing these standards, however, distracts our attention away from other dynamics. First, although only a very limited number of salaried positions exist, employees who are not promoted are framed as having not performed adequately. Second, certain factors, such as a college education, that are more likely to correlate with one's ability to meet such standards are more consistent with particular demographic categories, i.e., white and middle-class, which already enjoy greater amounts of social privilege. Through these "objective" criteria, Wal-Mart reproduces, rather than resolves, larger patterns of social exclusion.

Moreover, numerous lawsuits strongly indicate that promotion standards are not always applied evenly, due to either overt discrimination or, more commonly, to the ways that many of us reflexively associate qualities such as "leadership potential" with certain *types* of people, particularly men. Indeed, Betty Dukes' initial complaint stemmed from a comment made by her then-manager: "People like you don't get promoted." Though her manager did not clarify his remark, we, like Dukes, can easily imagine that her race and gender were possible "character defects" that interfered with her promotion. Though rarely cited as the formal reason for non-promotion, there is ample evidence of discrimination at Wal-Mart (Featherstone 2005a), and that sexist and racist thinking often explains structural inequality in terms of personal failure.

Wal-Mart's mobility narrative also does not address the fact that their business model depresses wages throughout the economy: most competitors have lowered wages in order to stay alive in Wal-Mart's shadow (Neumark, Zhang, and Ciccarella 2008; Graff 2006; Dube et al. 2007). The company's model also affects the supply chain. A new report [http://nelp.3cdn.net/5b7daf391f06aa 6413_qfm6bigxz.pdf] by the National Employment Law Project argues that Wal-Mart's squeeze has lowered wages and motivated a shift to temporary and immigrant labor throughout the "multilayered and hydra headed" supply chain (Cho et al. 2011, 2).

Wal-Mart is notable for their role in generating an economic underclass, and for their simultaneous—and almost unprecedented—insistence that they are a path to social mobility for their cherished associates. Most Wal-Mart associates are, by necessity, Wal-Mart customers; Wal-Mart's low wage model creates a captive audience of consumers who cannot afford to shop anywhere else. Betty Dukes remarked on Wal-Mart's practice of "setting up right in Poorville," even placing ads in the local paper when welfare checks were issued (Featherstone 2005b). Whether intentional or incidental, Wal-Mart's sales increase under grim economic circumstances, including the U.S.'s recent recession (Maestri 2008). Some have even argued that, in effect, Wal-Mart depends on poverty to grow (Featherstone 2005a; Collins 2006).

Wal-Mart's critics invite us to reflect upon the neoliberal perversion of the American Dream, in which the concentration of wealth at the top of our society corresponds with ever larger groups of ordinary citizens fighting for basic living standards at the bottom. Despite the fact that each of us knows scores of "deserving" people who remain in this ever-widening bottom, in spite of their hard work, we maintain a tenacious faith in upward mobility. In neoliberal times marked by downward mobility and growing economic disparities, most of us still believe in the possibility of the *climb* rather than the brokenness of the ladder. Wal-Mart's hopeful self-presentation fortifies the "cruel optimism" that leaves many of us attached to dreams of mobility, even as they become more impossible to realize (Berlant 2011).

For or Against Collective Empowerment?

Circulating reports about Wal-Mart's low wages fuel the ambivalence we feel toward Wal-Mart. While consumers appreciate EDLP, they are often simultaneously aware that the prices are virtually incompatible with the promise of liberal inclusion. These reports foster the nagging concern that Wal-Mart preys on a permanent low wage workforce, that they are an agent in the disempowerment of groups of people, e.g., racial minorities, women, and the less educated. These perceptions and doubts create problems as Wal-Mart seeks inroads with non-white communities and women in the U.S. and abroad. As an attempt to manage and contain this ambivalence, Wal-Mart projects an image of interracial and multicultural harmony, and has aggressively promoted itself as actively engaged in uplifting disadvantaged populations. Toward this end, in 2003, Wal-Mart created an Office of Diversity [www.walmartstores.com/Diversity/] aimed at streamlining the transition of minority employees into management, and mounted a more robust affirmative action program in 2005. Indeed, part of why Wal-Mart gained permission to expand into Chicago was because they agreed to hire women and people of color to build their stores.

And the company is not shy about showcasing their successes: in addition to the "leaked" video of their Hurricane Katrina relief efforts, when the contract for the construction of Chicago's first Wal-Mart store was awarded to a company owned by a local African-American woman, Wal-Mart took out a full-page ad in *Ebony* magazine.[24] Moreover, recent ASMs prominently featured entertainers of color, including Will Smith, the Black-Eyed Peas, Alicia Keys, Juanes, and Lionel Richie. A lengthy segment by Rosalind Brewer, the African-American female President and CEO of Sam's Club, at the 2012 ASM was followed by a video describing three African-American women—a grandmother, mother, and daughter—who were all Wal-Mart associates. These women described how the company had helped them to get ahead, one of them remarking: "It's a great company! What more could we ask for?" as if women of color had never asked for more from the company, and perhaps had no right to.

Just as Wal-Mart's victory in the Dukes case resurrected their image as a redneck—and legally untouchable—boys club, new corporate initiatives strike a decidedly feminist chord. The Global Women's Economic Empowerment Initiative [www.walmartstores.com/women/] highlights the company's efforts to promote women's employment on farms and factories, gender diversity in Wal-Mart accounts, job training and education for women, as well as sourcing from women owned businesses. This initiative was launched in 2011 and counts Secretary of State Hillary Clinton (the first female member of Wal-Mart's board) as a partner, signifying the potential to win over some of the store's more established feminist critics.

These philanthropic efforts and programs often depart from the neoliberal narrative of individual mobility in the sense that they single out women and minority groups for a helping hand. As was the case with Katrina, Wal-Mart frequently appears as a benevolent governmental agency tasked with helping disadvantaged groups *en masse*. But Wal-Mart's efforts are very selective. For example, if Wal-Mart is interested in "empowering" their global and primarily female supply chain workers, as well as the "disadvantaged" clients of Dress for Success, why does the company object to making life easier for their own associates? We believe Wal-Mart's resistance to unions or class actions constitutes a refusal to recognize their employees as a group whose self-defined interests diverge from their own and threaten their bottom line. This aversion toward contentious groups ultimately succeeded in the Betty Dukes case: while female associates remain free to sue Wal-Mart as individuals, their affiliation with a self-defined group, i.e., women who claim systematic discrimination, remains unrecognized.

Discrimination: Dukes and Beyond

In essence, *Wal-Mart v. Dukes* hinged on one very important disparity in the professional aspirations of Betty Dukes and her peers: between how high they *imagined* they could climb, and how high they (now) believe they were *allowed* to climb. The plaintiffs in the Dukes case alleged that female employees were systematically denied equal pay, promotions, and training. Many also claimed that they were subjected to workplace retaliation because of their gender. They argued that Wal-Mart's strong, centralized structure fosters or facilitates gender stereotyping and discrimination, that the policies and practices underlying this discriminatory treatment are consistent throughout Wal-Mart stores, and that this discrimination is common to all women who work or have worked at Wal-Mart. They argued that these acts of discrimination were a large part of why, although over 70 percent of Wal-Mart's employees are female, nearly two-thirds of its managers are male.

Lawyers representing these women argued that, in addition to the fact that their clients were singled out for different and inferior treatment because of their gender, they were also disadvantaged by a corporate culture that systematically holds women back. They claimed that Wal-Mart's family model of management relegated women to a complementary yet subordinate role; by deploying a family metaphor within the company, Wal-Mart's corporate culture naturalized the hierarchy between their (mostly) male managers and a (mostly) female workforce (Moreton 2009). The attorneys' argument was shaped by the case's expert witness: a sociologist named William Bielby who specializes in gender and workplace discrimination. Guided by a theory of "cognitive bias," Bielby determined that "subjective and discretionary features of the Wal-Mart personnel system created systematic barriers to the career advancement of women" (Bielby 2005, 395).

Wal-Mart's legal strategy was two pronged. First, they argued that the 1.6 million litigants were too diverse to constitute a "class"; second, they purported that the company was too de-centralized and the stores too diverse for that many women to have been so uniformly affected. In short, Wal-Mart argued that they were too big to be sued in a class-action lawsuit, one of the only legal strategies available to "ordinary" people who cannot afford to hire their own attorney. Although Wal-Mart ultimately prevailed, the door to collective action against the company is not completely closed. The company recently settled with a group of African-American truck drivers with similar claims of discrimination (Associated Press 2009).

The outcome of the Dukes case was predictably hailed and decried by various Wal-Mart proponents and detractors, but we are more interested in Dukes' strategy than in her defeat. By claiming that Wal-Mart imposed limits on their professional opportunities, Betty Dukes and her fellow litigants defined their ability to be "successful" in terms that were quintessentially American. By arguing that their presence near the bottom of a hierarchy was due to unfair treatment at the hands of sexist managers—and not to structural obstacles— the lawsuit affirmed the existence of a fair and functioning ladder to social mobility, a supposedly neutral standard by which many Americans gauge their individual success and self-worth.

Wal-Mart v. Dukes reminds us that discrimination remains an impediment to social mobility; the Supreme Court did not unanimously reject the plaintiffs' evidence, but rather could not agree on whether 1.6 million women suffered the same experience. But even if it had succeeded, the suit would have reinforced the dominant narrative of social mobility by positing the act of discrimination as the only barrier to getting ahead in the U.S.—an exception to the rule of equal opportunity. But structural impediments to social mobility do exist, even without discrimination. Even were Dukes victorious, it would not change the situation of a textile worker in Bangladesh, for example, who has been sewing garments for Wal-Mart's suppliers since the age of thirteen, and who might question Wal-Mart's "commitment to working women."[25] What do we imagine about these "supply chain workers" and how might they interpret the phrase "*Yes you can!*"—the phrase that Wal-Mart has asked them to sew into the lining of each and every suit jacket fashioned for Dress for Success, a jacket they cannot even afford? The idea of a ladder normalizes the belief that full citizenship can and must be earned, and that those on the bottom need only wait their turn. In this vision, someone is always, *necessarily,* on the bottom, working their way up. The detail that this vision obscures, however, is that some never even get a turn at all.

Conclusion

Wal-Mart spends millions in advertising telling the stories of Lyneese, Tejas, and Noemi in order to distract us from a low-wage, pyramid shaped, and patriarchal business model that preys on poverty and constrains real social mobility. But this ladder metaphor conveniently ignores the simple reality that "[s]omeone still ha[s] to stock the shelves" (Moreton 2009, 135), and that that someone is far more likely to be non-white, female and less educated. Stories about disadvantaged individuals successfully "climbing the ladder" limit our frame of reference to market based, individual models of advancement and relegate direct, collective, political efforts to resolve social hierarchies outside the realm of the thinkable.

Wal-Mart presents their path to social mobility as a cancelation of the debt they owe their employees for their hard work, as well as for a social debt created by historical injustice and present day discrimination. However, their repayment does not resolve inequality or poverty and tends to make these problems worse. Wal-Mart ignores how the question of debt is framed by their critics, including many of their own associates. Lawsuits like the Dukes case blame discriminatory treatment at Wal-Mart for preventing the ladder from functioning properly. Other critics emphasize how inequality is built into our society and how it has been exacerbated by free market policies. Many accuse Wal-Mart of spearheading these trends: fighting against living wages, benefits, and unionization, and sending a powerful ripple throughout the market. Many critics also emphasize the need for a significant redistribution of material resources in order to overcome social exclusion. Such demands and the groups that make them are rendered incoherent, invisible, or harmful in Wal-Mart's representational strategy, yet persist as a consistent reminder of the contradiction between the company's self-image as a social leveler, and the concrete effects of its business practices.

5

WAL-MART'S ANTI-UNION STRATEGIES

In June of 2011, a group of 100 former and current Wal-Mart associates visited the company's headquarters in Bentonville to ask for better treatment at work. Assembled under the name OUR Wal-Mart (Organization United for Respect at Wal-Mart) [http://forrespect.org/], the associates asked to meet with executive management in order to present a "Declaration for Respect," a list of nine requests that included predictable schedules and affordable healthcare[26] [http://forrespect.org/our-walmart/about-us/]. The group was met by Karen Casey, Senior Vice President of Global Labor Relations, who promised to listen to their concerns and that there would be no retaliation against the group's members.[27] The following October, several hundred members—along with a variety of supporters, including us—traveled to headquarters once again, and asked to meet with CEO Mike Duke. This trip to Bentonville was part of a two-day conference held in nearby Fayetteville, where members strategized with supporters about how OUR Wal-Mart could both grow as an organization and effect real change in their workplaces.

On this second visit, things did not go as smoothly. Though few members expected to obtain a meeting with Duke, the group was shocked and disappointed by Wal-Mart's harsh response. Upon their arrival at head-quarters, the group was quickly met by Wal-Mart security guards who not only disallowed entry into the building, but threatened to arrest anyone on company property who could not produce a Wal-Mart ID card. Sporting t-shirts in the group's signature chartreuse color, and carrying signs reading "I Want to Work Full-Time," "Stop Cutting Hours," and "We are Back, Demanding Respect," the group spent the next half-hour rallying on the sidewalk with supporters like Terry O'Neill, the president of the National Organization of Women [www.now.org/], and representatives of a national group called Making Change at Wal-Mart (MCW) (see Figure 5.1).[28] Girshriela Green, who had traveled from Southern California in order to participate in the meetings, told a reporter, "I feel totally disrespected. Shame on them for not having the

Figure 5.1 Members of OUR Wal-Mart protest at Wal-Mart home office in Bentonville, Arkansas. Photo by OUR Wal-Mart. Used with permission.

common decency to sit down and talk to their own associates" (Woodman 2012).

So what happened between June and October? This chapter will begin to answer that question by examining Wal-Mart's vision of labor rights, as well as how that vision is materialized in the company's labor management policies and practices. Since its inception, OUR Wal-Mart has received financial and organizational support from the United Food and Commercial Workers (UFCW) [www.ufcw.org/]. The UFCW, as Wal-Mart well knew, is a union that is fiercely interested in organizing Wal-Mart's associates as the company is in preventing them from doing so. "'The mission of the U.F.C.W.,' says one spokeswoman, 'is to raise standards for workers in the retail and grocery industry. [And y]ou cannot change the standards in the retail and grocery industry unless you also change Wal-Mart'" (Greenhouse 2011).

Given their centrality to the company's success, Wal-Mart's labor practices merit close scrutiny. Wal-Mart insists that its strict anti-union attitudes are mitigated by fair working conditions and a corporate culture of respect and openness that dissuade employees from seeking "third party representation." This narrative is complicated, however, by the millions of Wal-Mart associates who have sought or are seeking a collective voice through which to assert their grievances and requests—whether that be a website [www.walmartat50.org/]

or blog, a class-action lawsuit, a union, or a "non-union" like OUR Wal-Mart. Although Wal-Mart attempts to stop unionization through performances of family, belonging, and social mobility, they also rely—quite heavily—on a well-rehearsed and repressive set of anti-organizing strategies to keep their associates in line.

Managing Labor

In 2010, in the midst of the worst economic crisis since the Great Depression, Mike Duke earned $18.7 million and Wal-Mart cut 13,000 jobs. Such a disparity is consistent with a corporation like Wal-Mart's capitalist bottom line: maximize profits and reduce costs in order to make money for investors and executive bonuses. Low labor costs, the lowest in the business, is the most important factor in Wal-Mart's ability to deliver low prices. Labor costs are where management's zeal for efficiency is concentrated. This reality places the interests of managers and employees at odds in very fundamental ways.

In addition to the meager pay and notorious flexible scheduling, working at Wal-Mart is often stressful, physically demanding, and sometimes demeaning. It can be fast-paced and repetitive drudgery. The Bentonville office sets very high efficiency goals and maintains constant pressure on managers to "beat yesterday" in their sales to expenses ratio (Lichtenstein 2009), as well as to "do more with less." Though the pressure is grueling, managers who can withstand and meet these demands are ultimately rewarded—with promotions, a more consistent work schedule, a store closer to their family, and bonuses that push their salaries into the six-figure range. In contrast, managers who do not perform risk being fired or relocated away from their families, or to less desirable parts of the country.

Headquarters encourages managers to "be creative" about meeting productivity goals, leading to practices that often cross the line from demanding to illegal. Stores are often understaffed, which increases the responsibility and workload of each employee. Workers are frequently presented with three co-existing realities: the work must be done at the end of the day; overtime pay is unacceptable; and all employees can be replaced. In the past, this tactic has led many employees to work off the clock—some out of fear of being laid off or having their hours cut, others out of loyalty to a manager that they know would be sanctioned. Most managers now make it clear that they do not want employees to work off the clock, given that it is illegal and that reports of this practice caused a scandal, yet continue to make unrealistic demands on associates. Some managers have also been known to get "creative" with workers' time-sheets, redistributing their hours, for example, in order to make a week of overtime look like two weeks of part- or full-time work. Employees have reported being hounded by managers while on their breaks and being drug tested if there is any kind of accident or mishap in the store for which the company or manager may be held liable.

Employee Resistance to Wal-Mart

Not surprisingly, not all associates are as enthusiastic about Wal-Mart as their PR suggests. Many employees work at Wal-Mart as a simple means to an end, and even some loyal workers become alienated. Some aggrieved employees who find the "Open Door" closed or ineffective, or the ladder to success broken, turn to the legal system. Wal-Mart has been the focus of numerous wage theft lawsuits related to off-the-clock and other uncompensated work. With the corporate-friendly appointments to the National Labor Relations Board [www.nlrb.gov/] during the Bush Administration, Wal-Mart fought these suits in court. When President Obama appointed pro-labor Secretary of Labor Hilda Solis, however, Wal-Mart settled 63 of these lawsuits, paying out over $600 million in total (Lichtenstein 2009, 144). Individual lawsuits against Wal-Mart are difficult, however, as the company has both the time and the money to hold cases up almost indefinitely.

One way that employees resist managerial domination on a mostly individual basis is through stealing. Each year, approximately $30 billion worth of inventory "shrinks" away. A little less than half of this is from employees, who collude with friends to steal from the registers or to abuse Wal-Mart's "no questions asked" return policy. According to Lichtenstein, the number one cause of employee theft is related to a "sense of betrayal, of injustice, of taking what's due" (2009, 146) back from the company. Wal-Mart has a slightly lower percentage of shrinkage than other retailers due to an aggressive set of procedures that, at their most extreme, locked overnight employees into the stores.

Sam Walton set up a Loss Prevention department in 1973. This unit expanded throughout the 1980s and 1990s, growing into an agency that Lichtenstein claims instills fear among employees and managers alike. Now called "Asset Protection" (AP) the department is authorized to take over problem stores and fire managers and employees. In addition to running an intricate surveillance system, with security cameras throughout the stores and parking lots, the department polices the behavior of employees and managers; this extends especially to any activity suspected of being union-related. In 2002, after then-executive James W. Lynn spoke out against the labor practices he witnessed in some of the company's Central American supply factories, AP was sent to investigate not the labor practices, but *him*. Lynn was fired soon thereafter on charges of an improper romantic relationship with a female co-worker, with whom he was touring the factories (Greenhouse 2005; Meyerson 2005). He filed a retaliation lawsuit in 2005, but ultimately lost.

In the past decade, AP expanded even further to include a new organization called the "Threat Research and Analysis Group" to "spy on Wal-Mart's own employees and consultants, investigate hostile bloggers and activists, and keep tabs on the weak links in Wal-Mart's international supply chain" (Lichtenstein 2009, 151). One unintended consequence of theft is that through the drive to eliminate it, Wal-Mart has morphed into a highly integrated, powerful police apparatus that monitors customers as well as employees. Living in Northwest Arkansas, we have heard several friends and acquaintances who work for Wal-Mart say that they do not want to speak ill of the company because "you never know who is listening."

Another way that employees resist Wal-Mart's tactics is to quit, and each year, thousands do. Turnover hovers around 50 percent and reached an industry high of 70 percent in 1999, costing the company nearly $2 billion per year in training. Wal-Mart is largely unmoved by such rates. Unlike companies who might use them to catalyze retention strategies, Wal-Mart has incorporated these turnover rates into their business model [www.nytimes.com/packages/pdf/business/26walmart.pdf](Lichtenstein 2009, 135). Wal-Mart actually profits off of alienating workers. When workers do quit, perhaps their most active resistance toward the company, they often encounter an employment landscape shaped, at least in part, by Wal-Mart.

Zero Tolerance for Unionization

In Western societies, individuals are the focus of everything. Most of us are told that as individuals we can do anything, be anything. The dominant economic philosophy of our day tells us that selfishness and accumulation is the path to human freedom, prosperity, and happiness. We are also taught to think of our political agency as a series of individual, private, choices. But our political power is not limited to individual action. We are hardly aware that collective action is the most powerful force of social change on the planet. Collective—not individual—action is the primary way that humans make history. It toppled colonialism in Africa and South Asia and was the engine of the Civil Rights movements in the United States. Many of these movements demonstrated the power of non-violent collective action. The Arab Spring [www.aljazeera.com/indepth/opinion/2012/05/201257103157208253.html] is a recent and stunning example of ordinary people taking to the street to reclaim democracy and dignity in the face of oppression and what seemed like overwhelming odds.

Figure 5.2 Pro-union button.

Labor unions have been one of the most effective manifestations of collective action in the modern era. Without a doubt, the most powerful potential form of resistance to Wal-Mart's low wages and "people" policies is unionization. Unions not only represent the collective interests of workers, they constitute one of the only forms of power outside the company's control and the only check on management prerogatives. Unions can exercise their power through collective bargaining, work slowdowns, boycotts, and strikes. Contemporary union demands include a larger share of the company's profits, lighter and more realistic workloads, more predictable schedules, full-time employment, and overtime pay. In the past, they won many concessions that we now take for granted, like weekends, sick days, and the forty-hour work week.

The National Labor Relations Act [www.dol.gov/olms/regs/compliance/ EmployeeRightsPoster11x17_Final.pdf] of 1935 (also called the Wagner Act) granted workers the right to collective bargaining and was intended to allow employees to freely choose whether or not to form a union. The law also made it illegal to retaliate against or threaten workers with the loss of their job if they wanted to join; both these practices were labeled as unfair economic coercion. This New Deal law explicitly forbade bosses from taking a public stance regarding their employees' decision to unionize, on the grounds that any discouragement could constitute an implicit threat to workers' rights. This led to an upswing in union organization. The Taft-Hartley [www.nalc1414. org/Taft-Hartly.pdf] act of 1947, however, undermined many of the Wagner Act's provisions through numerous restrictive measures: prohibiting other unions to launch "sympathy" strikes or boycotts; passing *right-to-work* laws that allowed states to ban unions from collecting dues from non-unionized employees at unionized shops; and permitting employers to mount counter-union campaigns in the workplace, just to name a few.

Wal-Mart fears organized workers more than anything else, and derides unions as unnecessary intrusions, "third party representatives," and threats to their bottom line. This vehement opposition is because low cost labor is the crux of their low price business model. Wal-Mart emerged in the post-Depression south, where, in contrast to the industrial northeast, cultural opposition to unions was strong and legal protection for them was weak; this was due to the regional economy's historic reliance on cheap agricultural labor, and a longstanding fear of an African-American uprising (Lichtenstein 2009; Moreton 2009). Like most southern states, Arkansas's right-to-work law made it more difficult to organize a union. Throughout his career, Sam Walton routinely fought minimum wage laws and flouted labor laws (Lichtenstein 2009). To date, not a single Wal-Mart store in North America has successfully organized a union.

Wal-Mart claims that they are pro-associate, rather than anti-union, but internal company memos hint at a different story. In 1991, a branch manager at a Wal-Mart distribution center in Greencastle, Indiana, wrote an anti-union guidebook for supervisors entitled "Labor Relations and You at the Wal-Mart Distribution Center #6022." The author, Orson Mason, stated in no uncertain terms that "Wal-Mart is opposed to unionization of its associates. Any suggestion that the Company is neutral on the subject or that it encourages associates to join labor organizations is not true" (quoted in Lichtenstein 2009, 175–176). These attitudes have changed little, and they recently provided the tipping point for the largest pension fund in the Netherlands—Algemeen Burgerlijk Pensiofonds (ABP)—to divest over $120 million from Wal-Mart (Shapiro 2012).

Union Busting the Wal-Mart Way

When questioned about why Wal-Mart allows unions in their foreign stores, John Peter, "JP," Suarez, senior Vice President of International Business Development, replied: "We recognize those rights. In that market, that's what the associates want, and that's the prevailing practice" (Mui 2011). But the overwhelming force of Wal-Mart's anti-union strategy suggests that workers in the company's North American stores might also want unions—as did over 30 percent of the American workforce during much of the twentieth century—if given the freedom to organize. Wal-Mart deploys a multi-pronged and extremely aggressive anti-union strategy. Critics see Wal-Mart as one of the most anti-worker companies in the world, arguing that their union busting tactics create a very uneven playing field, effectively depriving their associates of the right to organize, and gutting the spirit, as well as the letter, of U.S. labor law.

Wal-Mart's approach to union busting, perfected over decades and costing the company billions per year, is both a science and an art. Between the 1970s and the 1990s, their response was shaped by Jonathan Tate, an anti-union lawyer and crusader who helped to institute several concrete measures to deflect union activity: profit sharing programs that allowed employees to cultivate a "stake" in the company; staving off union elections as long as possible; and adopting a zero tolerance policy against labor negotiations (Lichtenstein 2009, 162). Tate also recommended that Wal-Mart take their anti-union stance directly to the wider public through a public relations campaign.

From the moment an employee is hired, she or he is required to watch anti-union training videos in which unions are depicted as anti-democratic, authoritarian, and self-interested bullies who exist solely to leech off the efforts of working people. (Ironically, a company whose very purpose is to generate profits off their workers' labor criticizes unions for having the very same goal.) The videos allege that unions destroy jobs, rob workers of their freedom, and are anti-American. Wal-Mart's propaganda stresses that unions are unable to guarantee anything and that they will inevitably lead to conflict and strikes.

Managers are expected to study the "Manager's Toolbox," an anti-union training kit that teaches them how to preemptively respond to unions, identify pro-union applicants, and maintain morale. Steps toward achieving these goals include promoting the "Open Door Policy" and identifying early warning signs of union activity, including the "types" of employees predisposed to union rhetoric. Managers are also encouraged to monitor morale through meetings, surveys, evaluations, tracking the turnover rate, and a practice known as "Coaching By Walking Around (CBWA)"—i.e., watching and listening to employees. Employees known to be interested in labor organizing complain about the "unnecessary coaching" to which they are subjected. The Toolbox also coaches managers on how to respond to union activities, beginning with an immediate call to the company's anti-union hotline in Bentonville (where all union activity is monitored closely) (Wal-Mart 1997).

"Early Warning Signs" of union activity, for which managers are expected to look out, include things like: "increased curiosity in benefits and policies"; "associates receiving unusual attention from other associates"; "slowdown in work productivity"; mistakes; reports of employee conflict; and an increase in complaints and confrontations with management. More advanced signs include: "strangers spending an unusual amount of time in the associates' parking areas at the beginning or end of shifts"; "associates spending an abnormal amount of time in the parking lot before and after work"; "frequent meetings at associates' homes"; "associates coming back to the facility to talk to associates on other shifts"; "associates leaving work areas on a frequent basis to talk to other associates." The final stages, according to the Toolbox, include open signs of union activity such as literature, membership cards, and frank discussions about unions (Wal-Mart, 1997).

The "Early Warning Signs" tell us how Wal-Mart corporate management imagines the effects of unions on the workplace, and reveals a lot about the retailer's vision of an ideal employee. The ideal employee does not complain, never calls in sick, and always works hard and quickly. They neither argue nor overly-fraternize with other employees or managers, and they do not spend too much time in the bathroom. They would be unlikely to confront managers with a complaint, and they would never challenge the authority of a manager in front of other employees. They are also not looking for a sense of belonging with their peers, a "solidarity" based in their collective identities as workers. Rather, they are individuals who maintain a loyalty to the company first and foremost.

For Wal-Mart, these activities and employee characteristics serve not just as signs of union activity, but also as reflective of the negative attitudes and activities associated with the spread of pro-union thoughts, thoughts that must be monitored and ideally eliminated. Wal-Mart is interested in what Foucault (1979) called "docile bodies": industrious, loyal, obedient, and complacent workers. They prefer to deal with "individuals" rather than "collectives" or "associations" of employees, because individuals are easier to control. The only collective, non-individual feeling tolerated is the sense of belonging to the store; anything else is treated as a potential threat.

As soon as a union organizing effort begins in a store, Wal-Mart exercises their right to demand an election, rather than allowing a union to form from union cards signed by 30 percent of employees. They then use the delay to wage relentless information warfare, saturating the workplace with anti-union propaganda and deploying a labor relations team who implements an aggressive anti-union strategy. Labor relations holds near daily, quasi-mandatory store meetings detailing all the negative aspects of union organizing, showing anti-union films, and having employees walk past and read a "Wall of Shame" of headlines depicting union abuses. The team repeatedly reminds employees that Wal-Mart has the right to replace striking workers. Though it is illegal, the company has also been reported to fire "troublemakers," make threats and promises, and spy on employees (sometimes using the stores' surveillance cameras). Given that the penalties for these tactics are both weak and erratically enforced, Wal-Mart feels emboldened to push the legal limits (Bianco 2006; Human Rights Watch 2007). An OUR Wal-Mart member we spoke with during the 2012 ASM told us that he has been "written up" on three separate occasions and received unnecessary coaching since he became involved with the organization. He has worked for the company for 16 years and, prior to his association with OUR Wal-Mart, had never been sanctioned.

The primary effect of these tactics is that employees are subjected to a one-sided view of unions; many also feel intimidated to even learn about them.

Indeed, many workers have described a climate in which they fear for their jobs if they express any support for a union. "I remember my training . . . at Wal-Mart," said one ex-employee to us recently. "Unions were perceived as a monstrous threat to the company, and they made that very clear in the videos." Employees often become bitterly divided into pro- and anti-union camps, with anti-union employees, strongly backed by the company, virtually browbeating those that are in favor. The outcome is almost always a vote against unionization. Though many may have wanted to vote "Yes," they do not believe they are a match for a company of Wal-Mart's size and strength. Wal-Mart presents these outcomes in the terms of employee "choice," and declines to acknowledge this power imbalance. The truth is that many workers who vote "No" are simply intimidated and outflanked by Wal-Mart's relentless campaign.

In the few instances where unions have formed, Wal-Mart has engaged in extraordinary scorched-earth tactics. When meat packers organized in Palestine, Texas, Wal-Mart pushed the responsibility for meat cutting onto the suppliers, ending the in-store preparation of food altogether, a move that not only punished the newly-organized workers, but fundamentally changed the meat industry. In Jonquière, Canada, where the laws are much more favorable to union organizing, Wal-Mart simply shut down a popular store rather than allow a union that had been voted in to exist. This served as a threatening reminder to employees that Wal-Mart will not tolerate a union. It also stands in stark contradistinction to Vice President Suarez's earlier cited remark.

A 2007 report by the advocacy group Human Rights Watch [www.hrw.org/] concludes that though Wal-Mart "largely compl[ies]" with U.S. law, they nevertheless "create a work environment so hostile to union formation that they coercively interfere with workers' internationally recognized right . . . to organize" (5). Indeed, ABP, the Dutch investor group, divested because even after several meetings with Wal-Mart executives regarding labor rights complaints, they discovered a job posting on Wal-Mart's website for a new director of labor relations that included the phrase "support a continued union free workplace" as one of the listed duties. After meeting with representatives of OUR Wal-Mart in Arkansas, ABP believed Wal-Mart to be in violation of the third principle of the United Nations Global Compact, which calls on businesses to "uphold the freedom of association and the effective recognition of the right to collective bargaining."[29] Speaking to the press about their decision, the head of the pension fund remarked, "We felt that if the workers' aren't happy, then what does that mean for the company?" (Pot et al. 2011; Shapiro 2012).

Wal-Mart's anti-union stance, and the competitive edge that it provides, pressures other retailers and grocers to cut labor costs and fight off unions. Wal-Mart's entry into the California grocery market led unionized grocers like

Albertsons, Vons, and Ralphs (owned by Kroger) to refuse to negotiate with a UFCW campaign in 2003, dealing a blow to the union and forcing the workers to accept a two tiered benefits program (Lichtenstein 2009, 305–306). In the post-lockout agreement, new hires lost pension and health benefits. One result of decreased union leverage is declining membership across the board.

New Organizing Efforts

OUR Wal-Mart

Pro-labor groups have begun to focus on changing Wal-Mart's business practices in ways that go beyond in-store unionization. For example, employees organizing through OUR Wal-Mart are experimenting with a persuasion strategy that calls for the store to live up to its own stated principles. Having identified "respect for the individual" as one of Wal-Mart's "core values," OUR Wal-Mart is attempting to leverage that value against the company.[30] George Boston Rhynes, an OUR Wal-Mart associate, describes the group's thinking in this way:

> We are the very essence of making Wal-Mart the "all that it can be." These people are not agitators. . . . These people are not trying to destroy Wal-Mart. These people are not trying to tear down the dream, nor the very heartbeat of what Mr. Walton stood for. But they are trying to bring what we have lost, what has been lost by people who did not have, in their hearts, what Mr. Walton had for the American workers.[31]

For Rhynes, it is these employees—grievances and all—that represent the heart and soul of the company; they are the workers who hew closest to the core values upon which Wal-Mart was founded. They challenge the company to recommit to its principles, one of which was Sam's admonition to "listen to everyone in [the] company." With testimonials, organizing meetings, a dynamic website, and a series of public actions, OUR Wal-Mart is constructing a counter-narrative: speaking back to Wal-Mart's corporate leadership about the human cost of their business decisions. At present, group membership is limited to several thousand members. Members attribute these low numbers to fear of management retaliation, but insist that there is plenty of underground support, and that most associates who do not support the organization nevertheless share many of their frustrations and desire for better treatment.

We attended the strategizing sessions held in Fayetteville when OUR Wal-Mart made its second trip to the home office in October 2011. We also met

Figure 5.3 OUR Wal-Mart sticker on a street lamp in Fayetteville, Arkansas during the 2012 ASM.

with them in June 2012, when they were in town for the ASM. Both trips were facilitated by the UFCW (via the group known as Making Change at Wal-Mart) and another labor-rights group called Jobs with Justice. Local activists from the Workers' Justice Center [www.nwawjc.org/] in Springdale were also invited to attend, plan, and engage in the activities. At the sessions we attended in October, members generated and recorded lists of concerns and worked in small groups to develop specific suggestions of how their working conditions could be improved. OUR Wal-Mart's message is decidedly optimistic. Indeed, given the difficulties faced by these workers, as well as the tenor of October's sidewalk standoff, it is remarkable how hopeful and reform-oriented the group remains. We heard several OUR Wal-Mart members voice the nostalgia of their colleague George Boston Rynes, wishing that the company could return to what it was like when Mr. Sam was in charge. Although their optimism may be a bit rosy, their loyalty to the company's original values is evident.

Having publicly referred to them at least once as a "group of malcontents" (Shapiro 2012), Wal-Mart has declined to engage with the group on their own terms—as a *collective* with a set of legitimate and *shared* grievances against the company. In a coordinated event at the 2012 ASM, however, the company agreed to a set of individual "open doors" with approximately 20 members of the delegation. The managers listened, but at the time of this writing, OUR Wal-Mart's major concerns remain unaddressed.

Warehouse Workers United

In addition to working with in-store associates, labor activists have begun to organize workers in Wal-Mart-contracted warehouses. Warehouse Workers United (WWU) [warehouseworkersunited.org/],[32] a project launched in 2008 by a coalition of unions called the Change to Win Federation, has begun to target logistics workers in the massive shipping warehouses in the Inland Empire region of Southern California's San Fernando Valley. Warehouses in the Inland Empire process vast numbers of shipping containers from China and Southeast Asia each day. A report issued by the National Employment Law Project entitled "Chain of Greed" paints a grim picture of working conditions that it attributes to Wal-Mart's outsourcing practices, especially the way that they squeeze independent contractors (Cho et al. 2011). These warehouses are known to be increasingly dangerous places to work and many of those injured are denied workers compensation [www.dol.gov/dol/topic/workcomp/index.htm] claims. Though many of these workers do the same job for the same company every day, most are employed by one of several hundred temp agencies that offer neither benefits nor job security. Moreover, wage theft and illegal firings are said to be routine, leading to extreme vulnerability on the part of these workers. Many are Latinos and recent immigrants, including many who are undocumented, and are heavily exploited. According to the WWU's lead organizer, Nick Allen:

> These warehouses are as bad as it gets in terms of working conditions in America . . . Wal-Mart largely pioneered this system and still sets the standards. We feel it's important for the biggest player to be held accountable for the conditions in this industry. Our goal is to raise standards throughout the industry and bring workers from shitty, minimum-wage temp jobs to decent jobs.
>
> (Woodman 2012)

WWU initially attempted to organize workers from across the industry but in 2010 began to focus exclusively on Wal-Mart-contracted warehouses because of how "fundamentally [the company's] influence shapes the region" (Woodman 2012).

Competing Visions of Labor and Rights

In Wal-Mart's worldview labor is a commodity, and labor rights are ideally set by free market laws of supply and demand. If workers do not like a job or wage, the argument goes, they can search elsewhere for better conditions or compensation. Unions are not necessary in this understanding because employees themselves can make individual choices about whether or not to continue selling their labor at a particular wage. The assumption is that in the market, both employers and employees are individuals of equal power and rights who have decided of their own free will to meet on a level playing field— one buying labor and one selling it. For Wal-Mart, unions distort this free market model.

This idealized vision of market exchange misrecognizes the asymmetry between these groups—asymmetries of wealth and power that are largely the result of non-market forces. According to unions, the only way to compensate for this asymmetry is to allow workers to collectively pursue their shared interests. In this perspective, individual rights cannot be exercised when collective rights are ignored. Wal-Mart, a strangely powerful legal individual—a corporate "person" [www.thecorporation.com/]—would rather deal with workers as individuals, who can be more easily appeased or ignored.

Another major difference between Wal-Mart's and unions' conception of labor is that Wal-Mart sees labor as a commodity, while unions see laborers as intrinsically valuable—human beings who possess dignity, and who deserve a certain standard of respect and treatment. For example, although Wal-Mart may view "just in time" scheduling as a natural complement to "just in time" inventory, an important distinction between these two efficiency measures is that the latter deals with inanimate objects, while the former deals with human beings with feelings, personal lives, and physical limitations. Wal-Mart views the market as providing for basic standards of treatment, while unions warn that following the law of supply and demand without attending to asymmetries at play in the construction of the market frequently leads to severe abuses of workers' rights.

As we have mentioned, corporations describe unions as anti-democratic, because collective decisions can trump individual choice. This ignores the fact that collective action also increases the individual liberty of each member of the group, even if not all members agree with every aspect of what the group strives to attain. Collective rights and individual rights are not opposites, but complementary. Although Wal-Mart claims that unions are a distortion of the free market and a threat to individual choice, they do not apply a similar standard to themselves with regards to their size advantage, their sophisticated anti-union tactics, or their aggressive efforts to reorganize the legal and political field in their favor.

In other words, a major distinction between business and labor involves how each group conceives of its "bottom line." For business, this is defined by the absolute cost of an item—a line of inventory, manufacturing equipment, a benefits package, or a workforce. Labor, on the other hand, defines a bottom line as the minimum amount of wages and benefits a worker needs to earn in order to enjoy a particular standard of living. For example, OUR Wal-Mart frames their concerns in terms of respect and they focus on rights that they deem to be basic and fundamental. Many Wal-Mart shoppers are ambivalent about these issues because many have been exploited at one time or another, at the same time that they have heard of union benefits packages that seem overly generous. The question for many of us becomes: what is the minimum level of benefits that we think a working person should enjoy, and should we collectively strive to achieve that for all workers? Is such a worldview compatible with patronizing our local Wal-Mart?

One alternative vision of workers' rights has been framed around the concept of a "living wage." Though it is not uniformly defined, the term generally refers to a forty-hour per week wage that can comfortably cover the cost of housing, food, utilities, gas, and basic clothing. *Living* wage campaigns distinguish themselves from efforts to increase the *minimum* wage in that the former make explicit links between wages, worker dignity, and the variability of housing and other markets most relevant to daily life. The Universal Living Wage campaign [www.universallivingwage.org/],[33] for example, believes that full-time workers should not have to spend more than 30 percent of their income on rent or a mortgage.

The concept of a living wage is of vital concern for many Wal-Mart associates, many of whom are struggling to hold onto forty-hours of work a week. Given that up to 42 percent of the residents of homeless shelters are working,[34] and that many Wal-Mart workers are not working full time, and that full-time work at minimum wage does not guarantee housing, and that many Wal-Mart workers qualify for federal food stamps and children's health insurance, it is quite possible that many Wal-Mart employees are homeless or nearly so.

Reshaping the Political and Legal Field

Less than 7 percent of the national private workforce is unionized. This is largely a result of the outsourcing of manufacturing and the automation of the workplace. But, according to the group Human Rights Watch, (2007), part of this is due to "unbalanced U.S. labor laws that tilt the playing field decidedly in favor of anti-union agitation" (5). In this legal context, Wal-Mart is able to outmaneuver legal protections for labor. While Wal-Mart might argue that they are simply playing by the same rules as everyone else with regards to labor practices (and they are not the only anti-union corporation), the idea that the legal context exists independently of these companies' actions misrecognizes the amount of time, energy, and money that they invest in actively shaping the regulatory framework in ways that benefit their interests (Denniston 2011).

Many corporations, including Wal-Mart, lobbied hard to defeat the Employee Free Choice Act [www.govtrack.us/congress/bills/111/hr1409], which would have allowed employees to unionize when half of them signed union cards in any given workplace (rather than form through elections). Corporate influence over the regulatory system extends far beyond union law. The recent Supreme Court case, *Citizens United v. the FEC*, which allows corporations to donate freely and anonymously to political campaigns, promises to increase the influence that corporations like Wal-Mart exercise over politics. In 2011 and 2012, shareholders at the ASM voted down resolutions calling for greater transparency in the company's corporate donations. The Walton family also exercises a great deal of political influence, and works to disseminate a free market message as widely as possible. The family lobbied to end the estate tax, and the Walton Family Foundation [www.waltonfamilyfoundation.org/] has given large sums to charter schools and school privatization groups.

Another significant reason for American workers' decreased union participation is that propaganda campaigns like Wal-Mart's have been largely successful. Their perspectives have reshaped commonsense, which now holds that unions used to be necessary—a long time ago when things were really bad—but have since outlived their usefulness; today, in this narrative, they are little more than corrupt, greedy, and "job killing" organizations. Centrist and conservative outlets alike repeat anti-union propaganda in allegedly neutral reports that depict the decline in unionization as a matter of worker choice, without attending to the structural conditions (outsourcing, automation, and anti-union legislation) that contributed to the decline. Many of today's politicians and pundits blame unions, rather than industry outsourcing to find cheap labor, for the loss of U.S. manufacturing jobs. Union members and organizers are often depicted as "socialists," "thugs," and unpatriotic. In 2011, Republican governors in several states, most notably Wisconsin, fought to strip public sector unions of collective bargaining rights, blaming bloated union pensions for unsustainable budget deficits. This provoked a backlash in the form of mass protests and recall votes—against Governor Scott Walker as well as several members of the Wisconsin state senate. Although the recall of Walker failed, the popular uprisings that emerged around his anti-union activism resonated both locally and nationally, suggesting the possibility of a

6

THE SPACE OF
WAL-MART

A 2002 documentary titled *This is Nowhere* [www.highplainsfilms.org/hpf/films/this_is_nowhere] tells the story of a group of retired Americans spending their golden years touring the United States. Like many of their peers, these seniors are traveling across the country in the comfort of their "RVs" (recreational vehicles). The individuals profiled in the movie are regular and enthusiastic Wal-Mart customers, and use Wal-Mart parking lots as their overnight campsites—a practice the company explicitly encourages. Not only does Wal-Mart make camping permissible and free, they also publish a *Wal-Mart Atlas* to help RVers locate stores along their routes. The individuals featured in the film believe that the parking lots compare favorably to other RV campgrounds. Alongside feeling "welcomed with open arms," campers extol the company's ability to provide them with a laundry list of added benefits: extra security, needed supplies (such as toilet paper or a new toaster), the company of fellow travelers in the evening, and—perhaps most importantly—a reliable and delicious dinner at the end of a long day.

This is Nowhere presents viewers with an interesting juxtaposition: between the varied and at times extraordinary landscapes that surround these travelers by day, and the homogenous and prosaically-ordered expanses of asphalt upon which they spend their nights. By both waking up and falling asleep in these parking lots, the film's protagonists literally frame their days with Wal-Mart, a practice that some would say is a mere extension of the way that most Americans experience the company. Given that almost 90 percent of Americans live within 15 miles of a store (Basker 2007), we are hard-pressed to deny Wal-Mart's looming presence. Indeed, Wal-Mart's influence is so far-reaching, it is difficult to assert that we are living anywhere other than in what anthropologist and journalist David Moberg calls its "global shadow" (2011, A3). Not all of us, however, embrace this position wholeheartedly.

Each of the environments encountered by these travelers constitutes a place: an assemblage of (geographical) location, material form, and ascribed meanings

(Gieryn 2000, 463). Sociologist Thomas Gieryn suggests that space is doubly constructed: in addition to being "carved out" of material resources, places are simultaneously invested with meaning—"interpreted, narrated, perceived, felt, understood, and imagined" (465). As Wal-Mart expands, its effects on place are significant. Not only does the company shape the material form of the places it inhabits, it enshrines new meanings about those places, making specific experiences possible and eclipsing or eroding others. The spatial practices associated with big box discount shopping are also the focus of a range of political issues (e.g., zoning regulations, tax rates, appearance, traffic, and infrastructure) that are debated in city council meetings across the country.

This chapter examines some of Wal-Mart's place-making effects, and the politics of place in which it engages in order to gain entry into new spaces. We show how distinct social positions, occupied by a wide variety of social actors, contour the perceptions that individuals and groups have over whether and to what degree Wal-Mart "ruins" their landscape. We also demonstrate that the interpretations of several key terms—global, local, America, community, and environment—are profoundly shaped by those positions.

From Country Roads to Crystal Bridges

Although the company has since expanded well beyond its Ozark origins, Wal-Mart has stayed put in some noteworthy ways. Though executives and managers now travel on an increasingly global scale, the heart of Wal-Mart—its company headquarters and technology center—remain in Bentonville, Arkansas (see Figure 6.1) [www.bentonvillear.com/]. This means that vendors who want Wal-Mart to carry their products are pragmatically compelled to have at least a small office in northwest Arkansas, a practice that further solidifies Wal-Mart's relationship with its proverbial hometown. What this also means is that the formerly small town of Bentonville has undergone significant changes in its population (size and demographics), its physical structure (expansion, renovation, and new construction), and its economy.

These transformations have been of character as well as of scale. Many streets and buildings are named after the Walton family, including the Bud Walton Arena and the Walton School of Business, both on the University of Arkansas campus in nearby Fayetteville. Vendors and their families have moved from more densely populated, coastal, or more cosmopolitan cities, catalyzing significant changes in the local economy and the demographic profile of the region. The Northwest Arkansas metropolitan area, now home to nearly half a million people, ranks among the fastest growing regions in the U.S. The Bentonville-Rogers area is now home to a mosque, a synagogue, and a

Figure 6.1 The Wal-Mart home office in Bentonville, Arkansas.

Hindu temple—all founded primarily to serve Wal-Mart employees or vendors. An upscale outdoor mall called The Promenade, anchored by several national chain stores, opened in Rogers in 2003, and has become the area's most significant shopping destination. There is a regional airport in nearby Lowell with connections to major cities, and in 2011, the Crystal Bridges Museum of American Art (see Figure 6.2) [http://crystalbridges.org/] opened its doors to a highly enthusiastic and expectant public. Founded by Sam and Helen's daughter Alice, the museum contains one of the most important collections of American art in the United States and was endowed with an $800 million gift from the Walton Family Foundation, one of the largest gifts ever awarded to an American art museum. In an ironic twist, the company that used a local, country identity to export the model of ubiquitous retail culture to the rest of the United States (and now other parts of the world) is both directly and indirectly responsible for making their hometown more closely resemble the rest of the world.

Space-related issues have heated up since the late 1980s, when Wal-Mart began replacing their original discount stores with supercenters that combine both discount and grocery store inventories. Wal-Mart's real estate needs shifted

Figure 6.2 The Crystal Bridges Museum of American Art.

in response to this change, as the size of an average supercenter (187,000 square feet) is nearly double that of the earlier stores. The expanses of land likely to contain these parcels are more likely to be on the edges of town and are likely to cost significantly less. Though supercenters translate into a larger number of jobs—in both construction and permanent staffing—their space requirements generate a host of problems for community members, many of which are lumped under the term "sprawl."

The company now uses geospatial technology and monitors population growth patterns to determine locations for new stores. While acknowledging that their growth strategy is, at least in part, a response to shareholders' profit demands, Wal-Mart primarily narrates their expansion in the terms of its customer-driven mission: bringing the lowest possible prices to the greatest number of people. From this perspective, equal access to low-priced goods is equated with full citizenship and equivalent participation in the American Dream—"discount shopping [securing] parity with the freedoms affirmed by the Bill of Rights" (Bianco 2006, 169). When courting a new town (or nation), Wal-Mart's public relations team strives to present the store as universally acceptable and ideal for any locality. In addition to their famous prices, they promise governments and residents that they will increase the local tax base, create jobs, and positively contribute to community life.

But the company is aware that much of the public is ambivalent about its growth. Nelson Lichtenstein relates that in 1994, top executives discontinued the use of their "measles map" of the United States (in which a black dot stood for every existing store or distribution center) in the annual report distributed to shareholders. Though the map had been a point of inspiration as the company began expanding beyond the Ozark region, executives decided to drop it shortly after Sam Walton's death in 1992, during a period of massive growth and heightened public scrutiny. According to Lichtenstein, "as state after state became densely covered with scores of little black dots . . . a lot of people thought of the company's growth as something close to a cancerous malady corrupting the body. Why reinforce that imagery?" (2011a, A7).

Crashing the Gates

In the earliest days of the company, Sam Walton played hard-to-get: "feigning interest in potential store sites in towns adjacent to the one where he actually wanted to build" (Bianco 2006, 146) in order to secure subsidies like tax breaks and no-fee utility extensions. Though it has been decades since Wal-Mart needed this kind of assistance, the company continues to cajole cities and towns into providing it. These concessions often divert a limited pool of local funds away from public projects that may not otherwise survive. Given the company's enormous size and buying power, some critics argue that procuring these subsidies amounts to nothing short of extortion, an "unseemly racket [ill-suited to] a company that so loudly professes to have the best interests of everyday people at heart" (Bianco 2006, 146). Such allegations draw strength from Wal-Mart's tendency to leverage their potential capital against a community's economic need and vulnerability.

Wal-Mart also uses less-than-transparent real estate dealings, specifically their land acquisition and zoning circumvention strategies, to penetrate communities where there is organized opposition. Bill Quinn describes a variety of "sneaky ways" they use to get into a city under the radar. One of these, what Quinn calls a "front man," (2005, 36) refers to Wal-Mart's tendency to use a real estate or development company—that is either owned or contracted by Wal-Mart—to request rezoning or to make the initial purchase or lease in contested areas. These "shadow" entities allow Wal-Mart to both hide in plain sight, while simultaneously extracting the financial incentives for which the company is legendary.

Such opaque real estate practices also allow Wal-Mart to abandon buildings as routinely as they build them, creating unanticipated eyesores of convenience.

Converting to a supercenter or even an "express" store to meet the needs of a particular town or neighborhood often means closing down an existing discount store. Rather than leasing or selling the space to a competitor, and risk losing market share, Wal-Mart holds on to the building and leaves it empty (Bianco 2006, 151; Karjanen 2006, 157). Anti-Wal-Mart forces seize on these shells as additional proof of Wal-Mart's necrotic effect on the lived environment.

For many, the buildings themselves—even when occupied—provoke concerns about what having a Wal-Mart *says* about the neighborhood, and about the people who live there. These worries express the cultural politics of diverse groups. Many detractors think that "big-box" stores constitute a visual blight. Their conception of environmental dystopia is dominated by "the classic Wal-Mart square, prefab, ugly monstrosity of a building surrounded by asphalt parking lots as far as the eye can see" (Quinn 2005, 28). For some, the uniform corporate landscape epitomized by Wal-Mart dislodges us from our home-centered roots and leaves us floating through a series of reassuring but indistinguishable "nowheres"; these critics fear the erasure of a "homegrown" specificity, and bemoan what they see as the demise of community relations.

David Karjanen (2006) argues that corporate globalization has disrupted the "spatial stability" of earlier modes of capitalist exchange, in which workers purchased homes in the same towns as their company headquarters and shopped for goods that were manufactured by their neighbors. For Karjanen, companies like Wal-Mart have erased the "spatial environment . . . that puts workers, consumers, and capitalists in contact" (2006, 162) with one another. Much of this nostalgia, i.e., for "lost" communities, face-to-face relationships, and neighborhood familiarity, however, glosses over the racial exclusions and gendered and class-based hierarchies upon which these communities were often founded.

For some of these critics, large retail chains and the strip malls that they anchor function not only as an aesthetic assault and a blow to local home values, but also as a sign of the advance of crass "low culture." The acronym NIMBY, meaning "Not in My Backyard," describes the opposition—often associated with wealthy and powerful neighborhoods, towns (or even countries) —to undesirable, dangerous or otherwise distasteful development projects, such as a toxic waste dump, homeless shelter, low income housing, or a big-box retail strip mall. These different attitudes, and the political clout of the groups they represent, influence where physical structures are ultimately built. Some anti-Wal-Mart sentiment concerns the type of clientele—often poor and non-white—that a Wal-Mart store might attract, a group of consumers deemed threatening to dominant neighborhood identities and property values. These concerns have endured since the days that Sam Walton was expanding into rural county seats. Middle-class shop owners feared not only for the integrity of their businesses, but also that a Wal-Mart would bring seedy country folk to town.

Opponents of all stripes have reinforced their respective arguments with the hard facts: the econometric data that, although somewhat mixed, paints a fairly negative portrait of Wal-Mart's impact on a community. Researchers began "running the numbers" in earnest in the 1980s and many have demonstrated what Anthony Bianco (2006) calls the "ruinous volume of business [taken] away from competing merchants," and the "utter collapse of Mom and Pop retailing" (145). Agricultural economist Kenneth Stone provided some of the earliest—and most often cited—figures detailing this trend, based on survey data gathered in the state of Iowa. Wal-Mart opened 45 stores between 1983 and 1993; Stone found that during that time, "the state lost 555 grocery stores, 88 department stores, 298 hardware stores, 444 apparel shops, 293 building supply stores, [and] 511 other retail outlets—as much as 43 percent of some categories of retail stores" (Stone 1995; cited in Moberg 2011, A4).

Using data from national retail registers, economist Panle Jia (2007) demonstrated that Wal-Mart alone was responsible for a 50–70 percent decline of small discount retailers between 1988 and 1997 in any given area, while Emek Basker (2005) concluded that approximately four small competitors—in grocery, apparel, and retail—closed their stores within five years of Wal-Mart's arrival in a county. Basker suggests that Wal-Mart's effect may be "minor," given that there are up to 200 stores per county, but, in a separate study, he reports that stores who manage to stay open often experience a significant reduction in revenues—up to 17 percent (2007). More recent data from Stone and colleagues (Stone et al. 2002) suggest that local businesses can survive if they successfully distinguish themselves from a Wal-Mart store, e.g., through "handl[ing] different merchandise" and cultivating "niche markets" (27). However, limiting the scope of their study to one Wal-Mart in Chicago, Davis et al. (2009) found that almost one-quarter of businesses within four miles of the store had closed within two years of its opening.

As statistics like this became widely available, and the real world-impacts that they represented became increasingly undeniable, community resistance to the company flourished, spawning a generation of anti-Wal-Mart activists. Many "ordinary" people—even previously apolitical or conservative ones—felt compelled to educate themselves about zoning laws, land use ordinances, tax abatements, municipal bonds, and the inner-workings of their local governments. This led to organized opposition—demonstrations, petitions, books, documentaries, and the launching of anti-Wal-Mart websites—whose cumulative effect presented obstacles to the company's North American expansion. Several towns successfully blocked stores from opening; others slowed down or minimized the accompanying sprawl. These forms of opposition prompted the retailer to develop aggressive new legal, public relations, and architectural strategies to facilitate their entry into restricted markets. Some stores, for example, are now designed to occupy 99,000 square feet in order to circumvent big-box specific zoning laws that ban the construction of stores whose square footage exceeded 100,000 (Quinn 2005).

Most of these opponents focus on the specific problem of sprawl, the unchecked expansion of monotonous urban space that for many has become synonymous with Wal-Mart. Common objections focus on the material realities of big-box retail: expanded roadways and parking lots; transportation logistics and traffic congestion; industrial pollution and waste; and sometimes the declining property values of homes near the proposed development. Anti-Wal-Mart protesters attempt to persuade local politicians and voters that the externalities, or "hidden costs," of expansion are higher than the promised wages and tax revenues. Statistical analyses are reinforced by anecdotal horror stories demonstrating the disastrous effects of Wal-Mart on local economies. For many of these detractors, Wal-Mart-anchored retail sprawl ultimately means losing a dynamic and differentiated local economy to an international conglomerate whose attachment to any one "place" is dictated by profit margins rather than personal relationships, and by shareholder value rather than local ties.

Improving the Neighborhood?

Sam Walton claimed to have no interest in building where he wasn't wanted, but the company is frequently accused of "bullying" its way into localities, particularly those that have made their opposition to Wal-Mart known. But when "Mr. Sam" expressed this sentiment, the company was a great deal smaller; many of the cities and towns that played host to his new stores and supercenters had yet to experience two of the things for which a new Wal-Mart store has since become famous: disruption of the local economy and vehement disagreement between residents about what that disruption "means." Many of these "site fights" turn on issues of space: who gets to use it, for what purpose(s), what is it worth, and who will suffer and/or enjoy the consequences of its (re)development?

One of Wal-Mart's primary tactics in addressing local opposition is to circumvent City Councils and zoning boards entirely and take their case "straight to the people" via petitions and ballot measures. These "popular" referendums, however, are far from the straightforward "up or down" approval ratings that Wal-Mart would have its critics believe; rather, they are aggressive, carefully orchestrated, and well-financed public relations campaigns conducted in the style of Wal-Mart's anti-union activities. This PR sophistication is currently on display in New York City where Wal-Mart has launched a website called *Wal-Martnyc.com* [http://nyc.walmartcommunity.com/] whose purpose is to "separate the facts from the fiction" about the company's reputation and intentions. Wal-Mart promises to meet the real needs of city residents for cheap groceries and jobs, and downplays and denies the negative consequences of their arrival.

Critics also accuse the company of using "Wal-Mart math" (Norman 2004): taking credit for creating jobs and revenue without calculating what a store's arrival will cost. Seasoned opponents argue that because the final tally is usually "a wash" (Davis et al. 2009), Wal-Mart should not be awarded financial incentives to build. "They will promise you everything under the sun," said a former Wal-Mart grocery manager—turned anti-Wal-Mart activist—as she talked with a group of New Yorkers considering whether to oppose the store slated for their city; "but at the end of the day," she continued "they will take it all back" (Featherstone 2011, A20).

One well-rehearsed Wal-Mart narrative strategy plays on the so-called "elitism" of the company's critics, and emphasizes the real value that a Wal-Mart store brings to people from all walks of life. In the wake of the company's initial rejection from Los Angeles, then-CEO Lee Scott said this to a reporter:

> You have someone who says "My vision of the world does not include a large retail store—it is small shops with lots of trees out front and little parking spaces and individual owners." That may be a nice dream. Unfortunately, . . . [i]f you are a working person—if you are one of the twenty percent of Wal-Mart's U.S. customers who don't even have a checking account and you live paycheck to paycheck—that vision of the world may not be one that you can afford. If you are a working person and you need to save money, Wal-Mart is a great thing for you.
>
> (cited in Humes 2011, 50)

While this characterization may apply to some, it does not represent those who accuse the company of cutthroat capitalism, who view Wal-Mart as little more than an anti-union, anti-worker behemoth that proffers low-quality merchandise, lowers local wages, and drives jobs out of the country.

When building in more affluent areas, however, Wal-Mart's strategy is to cater to these "elitist" aesthetic demands. Wal-Mart has developed the "Neighborhood Market" [www.walmartstores.com/AboutUs/7606.aspx] as a twenty-first-century alternative targeted to upscale markets. With a forest green/earth tones color scheme, an average area of just 42,000 square feet, and a focus on fresh produce and basic necessities, the Neighborhood Market's aesthetic sensibility more closely resembles a Whole Foods Market than a Walton's Five and Dime.

Figure 6.3 The first Wal-Mart on Campus, at the University of Arkansas in Fayetteville.

Wal-Mart also understands that a willingness to adapt their stores—in both design and size—is a key factor in their ability to enter densely populated cities like New York, San Francisco, and Chicago. The first convenience-store sized Wal-Mart Express debuted in 2011 in Chicago and nine more opened within the year. The small format also allows the company to court college campuses. The Wal-Mart on Campus at the University of Arkansas in Fayetteville was also built in 2011 and is ripe for replication. Hip, scaled-down, and tailored to the needs of a dorm dweller, the store features plenty of prepared and microwave-able food, printer cartridges, contraceptives, and margarita mix. Additionally, an on-site pharmacy has replaced the one formerly housed in the student health center.

At 3,500–4,000 square feet, these stores are microscopic supercenters—so comparatively small in size that one journalist has already mused about "an ever-expanding proliferation of smaller and smaller Wal-Marts, until each of us has a miniature Wal-Mart in our own homes" (Northrup 2011). But whether tiny Wal-Marts constitute *evolution* or simply old-style *growth* remains to be seen. One research analyst, interviewed by a reporter in San Francisco, summed up Wal-Mart's plans to open two dozen Express stores in his city this way: "They're going after the urban market . . . [because] that's where the money is."[35]

Wal-Mart's Urban Frontier

With suburban locations nearly saturated, it is clear that Wal-Mart needs to conquer the urban market if they are to keep pace with their previous growth in the U.S. Their strategy thus far has been to emphasize not only their ability to "downsize" stores as needed, but also to create jobs, stimulate local economies, and provide access to affordable merchandise, particularly fresh food and produce.

Urban anti-Wal-Mart groups have had more success in opposing new stores primarily because major urban areas contain well-established, often thriving economies; these factors are often complemented by a higher concentration of liberals and non-whites who neither identify with the store's Southern, rural, and Christian image nor approve of their labor and sourcing practices. Opposition campaigns have been particularly successful in New York City where, early in 2011, the city council was forced to reschedule an economic impact hearing about Wal-Mart in order to accommodate the hundreds of people that wanted to speak (Herman 2010). Some urban Wal-Mart opponents have drawn upon the arguments presented by neighborhood activists and academics about the effects of big box and strip mall zoning on the spatial politics of inclusion and exclusion. These critics call attention to the ways that social hierarchies are lived through and in relationship to space; peoples' access to concrete spaces to live, work, and move about freely (without being sexually harassed or racially profiled, for example) is intimately bound up with the categories through which we organize and rank one another, such as gender, race, class, and ability. Many fear that Wal-Mart's presence will disrupt urban neighborhoods, displace minority-owned businesses, and exacerbate unemployment.

Food Deserts

As a specific response to these critics, Wal-Mart has begun to fashion itself as a solution to the problem of food deserts plaguing urban areas. Over the past decade, urban planners, local activists, and critical geographers have used GIS technology, along with neighborhood-based survey and interview data, to map out the phenomenon known as food deserts: parts of the country—both rural and urban—where people experience physical and economic barriers to healthy and affordable food (Whitacre et al. 2009). Research demonstrates that the frequently poor residents of these communities often solve their food-related needs in a variety of economically unsustainable ways, including shopping at high-priced convenience stores and using expensive cabs to access the lower prices available at larger stores. In a "major initiative" launched in January, 2011, with the support of First Lady Michelle Obama, Wal-Mart listed "[p]roviding solutions to ... food deserts by building stores in underserved communities" as the fourth of five primary goals intended to "make food healthier and [to make] healthier food more affordable."[36] Because income, race/ethnicity, and geography correlate so highly in the contemporary United States, the groups most likely to be affected by high prices and food deserts are African-American, Latino, and immigrant. By presenting themselves as food desert activists, Wal-Mart is able to accuse anti-sprawl activists of an elitist—even racist—agenda that disproportionately impacts people of color.

The concept of food deserts, developed by researchers and validated by techno-spatial data analysis, adds a scientific twist to a longer-standing strategy of Wal-Mart—that of utilizing racial identity politics to justify its erratic and not always successful urban expansion efforts. In 2006, Andrew Young, an African-American civil rights activist and former mayor of Atlanta, was the spokesman of a community organization called "Working Families for Wal-Mart" (the group was quietly funded by Wal-Mart) that lobbied urban minority communities to support the company. Young's brief stint as Wal-Mart's advocate ended when a reporter from the *Los Angeles Sentinel* asked him what he thought about local activists' concerns about Wal-Mart's adverse effect on local businesses. Young replied by saying, "You see, those are the people who have been overcharging us, and they sold out and moved to Florida. I think they've ripped off our communities enough. First it was the Jews, then it was the Koreans, and now it's the Arabs" (Barbaro and Greenhouse 2006).

By enlisting the support of a prominent African-American figure to target "working" rather than "black" families in their campaign, Wal-Mart hoped to indirectly gain the economic and ideological backing of racial minority groups who might otherwise perceive the company in negative terms. Although Wal-Mart immediately denounced the comments, and the group soon disbanded, the incident illuminated Wal-Mart's implicit conflation of race and class in their urban expansion strategy. Having recovered from the Young scandal, Wal-Mart is resurrecting their strategy, hoping that food deserts, which easily code for "race" and racially-linked poverty, will help them court urban minority communities. These tactics appear to have been successful in Chicago, where the retailer has gained the support of several prominent figures in the African-American community, as well as Mayor Rahm Emanuel.

This carefully crafted tale of Wal-Mart's free market heroism requires further scrutiny, however. Food deserts partially emerged out of the complex social phenomenon of "white flight" [http://mappingdecline.lib.uiowa.edu/map/]

to the suburbs in the post- Civil Rights era. African-Americans and other racial minorities remained in the cities, which quickly deteriorated. The combination of a weak tax base, racism, and inadequate public and private investment led to the "ghetto-ization" of many inner-cities in the U.S., a situation exacerbated by the drug trade and the federal government's "war" on it, which has remained fairly intractable for several decades. And though a new Wal-Mart might effectively "solve" the dearth of low-cost shopping and high-quality produce in some neglected neighborhoods, it does little to ease the larger burdens of poverty associated with this history. Indeed, some of these more persistent problems—such as depressed wages and lack of healthcare—are explicitly linked with the company's business model and its community-wide impact.

Another possibility is that a new supercenter or Neighborhood Market might gentrify [www.cdc.gov/healthyplaces/healthtopics/gentrification.htm] an area where Wal-Mart claims to be solving a food desert. As more affluent groups move *back* into inner cities following reinvestment, they inevitably drive up rents and property taxes, leaving low-income residents with fewer and fewer housing options. This was the case in New Orleans in 2001 when, prior to their heroic efforts during Hurricane Katrina, local activists accused Wal-Mart of preying on the derelict St. Thomas housing project set for "renovation" in the Garden District.[37] Though residents and the city were promised that the redevelopment would be mixed-use, allowing for the resettlement of previous residents alongside the retail that included the supercenter, opponents maintain that fewer than 100 of St. Thomas' 1,500 families were able to move into the neighborhood under its new name—River Gardens.[38]

Wal-Mart's urban presence may solve an immediate food desert "crisis" but the company's interest in urban areas could be driven by a desire to capture the future business of a growing segment of upwardly mobile urbanites. Instead of resolving the problem of inequality, Wal-Mart's partial solution might actually make the situation worse. If the problem cited by the term food desert is a lack of access to fresh, affordable, and healthy food, is a Wal-Mart supercenter a better solution than a community garden or a sustainably funded food bank, both of which have been shown to reduce grocery prices (Winne 2008; Larsen and Gilliland 2009)? Moreover, if food deserts are a symptom of poverty and other forms of social exclusion, perhaps a more integrated solution that begins to address those relationships is in order.

Community Benefit Agreements

In a growing number of U.S. cities, local activism has generated several types of compromises between businesses, local governments, and workers-rights advocates that are motivated by a human-rights framework. One of these is the business assisted living wage (BALW). Generally passed in the form of a local ordinance, BALW laws require that businesses participating in publicly-subsidized projects pay their workers with wages above the poverty level (Lester and Jacobs 2010). Research has demonstrated that not only do these laws have little to no impact on driving potential businesses away from a given area, they are also likely to increase local revenue because low-income wage earners spend a greater portion of their paycheck in their own communities (Schmitt and Rosnick 2011).

A compromise with a more comprehensive vision is known as the Community Benefits Agreement (CBA) [http://communitybenefits.blogspot.com/]. An almost direct response to Wal-Mart and its big-box brethren, CBAs attempt to hold large corporations responsible for the havoc they wreak on the geographical, business, and interpersonal environments of the communities in which their stores are located (Salkin and Lavine 2008). By establishing contracts between developers and communities, CBA's attempt to "ensure that development is equitable and benefits *all* members of the community, eventually contributing to stronger local economies, livable neighborhoods and increased public participation in the planning process."[39] They do this by requiring corporations to make clear up front what their store or business will do for the community. Expected benefits include, but are not limited to: a living wage, local hiring, training programs, environmental remediation, public transportation subsidies, donations to local organizations, and other community-specific programs or projects.

At least two cities—Washington DC and Chicago—have signed CBAs with Wal-Mart thus far; in the case of Washington, DC, the agreement [www.scribd.com/doc/73502937/Wal-Mart-Community-Benefits-Agreement] has been called "unprecedented" because the company is not requesting any local tax abatements or subsidies. In both cities, the CBA's include wage scales that resemble a BALW, and a commitment to hire local workers in the construction and staffing of the new stores.

Conclusion

Some neighborhoods and towns have a Wal-Mart but do not want it, while others want one but do not (yet) have one. Still others have a Wal-Mart and very much want to keep it. For many communities, a store's arrival means access to a wide range of merchandise and groceries, at lower prices than they have been paying, and a link to the mainstream. Many people view anti-Wal-Mart activism as a sign of the disdain that overeducated and liberal urbanites feel toward rural whites. Many, perhaps most, Americans are ambivalent and feel a bit of all of this. Indeed, even those who oppose Wal-Mart's expansion on aesthetic, social, or political grounds find the lure of low prices and one-stop shopping impossible to completely resist. Some residents who have successfully fought off Wal-Mart's arrival in their town now drive to neighboring towns in order to shop there.

Wal-Mart's expansion has embroiled the company in the politics of race, class, and community, with profound implications for the way that Wal-Mart situates itself into spaces. While the company leans on its power to enter localities, it relentlessly presents its expansion in a positive light. Wal-Mart works hard, and often successfully, to either dismiss its critics as elitists, or to outmaneuver them by presenting itself as a free market solution to social problems. However, Wal-Mart's assertive growth has given rise to new forms of citizen activism that attempt to tame the retailer by advancing a regulatory framework rooted in a distinct conception of human rights, one that places community over profit. As Wal-Mart continues its push into urban areas in the U.S. and around the world, these conflicts are likely to intensify.

7

WAL-MART
AT LARGE

Globalization refers to the movement of capital, people, commodities, ideas, feelings, and practices across national borders. And though human history is filled with these encounters—even before the concept of nations existed—they have increased in both speed and volume in recent decades. This has largely been due to advances in communication and transportation technologies through which time and space have become compressed (Harvey 1989), as well as to new regulatory frameworks that allow capital to move more freely across borders. Since the end of the Cold War [www.bbc.co.uk/history/worldwars/coldwar/], impediments to capital flows have steadily evaporated. American multinational corporations have spearheaded this process in their search for inexpensive raw materials, cheap and compliant labor, and new markets, enabling the American Dream to become a globally circulating imaginary. Neoliberals see globalization as the inevitable advance of freedom and the culmination of world history. Critics warn, however, of the flattening of cultural difference, planetary destruction, and the violent imposition of free markets on vulnerable populations (Hardt and Negri 2000; Stiglitz 2002; Harvey 2007). Wal-Mart exemplifies both the promise and the perils of neoliberal market integration, and thus provides an ideal vantage point from which to critically examine the optimistic rhetoric of globalization.

Global market integration is the crux of the neoliberal progress narrative and Wal-Mart is one of the most powerful corporate entities involved in bringing that story to life; not surprisingly, Wal-Mart is also one of globalization's largest beneficiaries. Wal-Mart institutes a specific model of globalization and, more than any other company (and most countries), it defines the terms through which globalization is conducted: directly negotiating ground rules with foreign governments and setting the trends for the company's multinational competitors. An integral element of Wal-Mart's success is their ability to maintain and expand their supply of inexpensive goods. Wal-Mart acquires inventory from factories all over the world, but 70 percent of their merchandise comes from China. In 2004, 10 percent of all Chinese exports to the U.S. went directly to Wal-Mart (Fishman 2005, 103), and Wal-Mart sources products directly and indirectly from over 10,000 Chinese suppliers (Chan and Unger 2011; Chan 2011). Global sourcing translates into enormous profits for companies like Wal-Mart: they pay pennies an hour for products that can be marked up a hundred or even a thousand percent in the U.S. and elsewhere. Wal-Mart's success also depends upon increased expansion into foreign retail markets. To this end, they have opened 5,651 stores in 26 countries [www.Wal-Martstores. com/AboutUs/246.aspx] outside the U.S.; these operate under dozens of local names and employ some 780,000 employees.[40] The company runs over 2,000 stores in Mexico alone.

Wal-Mart emphasizes the benefits that free markets and foreign competition bring to workers and customers worldwide and depicts their foreign expansion as a mutually beneficial exchange between cultures. The company also claims that their entry into poor countries will create jobs, improve women's lives, decrease food costs, and increase food security. They present their decision to outsource production and to open stores abroad as natural and inevitable: an almost evolutionary response to a global demand for their products, and a step toward overcoming international inequalities. In Wal-Mart's imaginary, they are helping to bring the American Dream to a world that is eager to "live better."

At the 2011 ASM, CEO Mike Duke proudly proclaimed that "the culture of Wal-Mart can work among the cultures of every country." Contrary to Wal-Mart's narrative, there is nothing inevitable or natural about globalization, or about the manner in which the company has pursued it. Nor is the company's business model universally compatible, as they claim. In this chapter, we highlight Wal-Mart's global strategy, particularly how they portray themselves as a free market solution to the persistent problems of poverty and inequality that plague the formerly colonized countries in the global south—Latin America, Africa, and Southern Asia. Wal-Mart's optimistic narrative of globalization ignores the historical production of these social problems, masks the ways that their global expansion capitalizes on and reproduces them, and renders local forms of resistance and structural political alternatives invisible. Though bringing no benefit to the company, we suggest that these other solutions might be more suitable and sustainable for populations who define "living better" outside of market logic, and for whom Wal-Mart's vision of the Dream has become a nightmare.

Looking for the World's Cheapest Labor

Wal-Mart imports billions of dollars' worth of merchandise, enough to fill hundreds of thousands of shipping containers from mainland China each year.

China was an early favorite source of manufactured goods because it had what Lichtenstein refers to as the perfect mix of factors: "stable currency, developed infrastructure, political reliability, and a compliant workforce" (197). Crowded, smoggy Chinese factory cities churn out inexpensive, high-volume items—often faithful copies of products once made in America—to Wal-Mart's EDLC specifications (Chan and Unger 2011).

Though Wal-Mart orders more products from China than any other U.S. company, its relationships with foreign-owned factories do not stop there—in Central America, South Asia and other parts of the global south, tens of millions of international supply chain workers move to the fits, frenzies, and starts of Wal-Mart's just-in-time ordering. In most of these countries, grinding poverty coerces workers into toiling for unthinkably low wages and in appalling conditions. Critics label these outsourcing practices a global "race to the bottom," as poor countries compete with one another for the least expensive production costs. Indeed, Chan and Unger (2011) conclude that Wal-Mart has already lowered wages in China. In economic parlance, poor countries offer a "comparative advantage," in that labor is cheap and regulations (e.g., regarding pollution) are lax. Wal-Mart converts these savings into shareholder value and EDLP, putting the material trappings of the Dream within reach for consumers.

While many of us may assume that Wal-Mart has always sourced its products from foreign factories, there was a time during the 1980s when they felt pressure from U.S. unions to do otherwise. During their "Buy America" campaign, Wal-Mart committed itself to "converting" products made offshore to American-made ones, though they used the specter of outsourcing to pressure American manufacturers to become more price competitive. The campaign initially helped Wal-Mart to project a more patriotic image but it came to a disgraceful end in 1992, when the television program *Dateline* revealed to the nation [http://findarticles.com/p/articles/mi_m3092/is_n2_v32/ai_13364723/] that many of Wal-Mart's products with a "Made in USA" label were actually made in China, Malaysia, and Bangladesh by children working under deplorable conditions.

Betting on Americans' preference for low prices over workers' rights, Wal-Mart chose to abandon the "Buy America" campaign rather than rehabilitate it. Since then, outsourcing has become the norm. Though the company claims to now be guided by a robust Ethical Standards Program,[41] critics maintain that Wal-Mart oversees one of the worst retailer supply chains in the world. Non-governmental monitoring organizations (NGOs), journalists, and academic researchers regularly report the following conditions: underpayment and stolen wages; 15-plus-hour work days with no overtime pay; dangerous and fast-paced work; inadequately ventilated workplaces; child labor; sexual harassment; daily pregnancy tests and firing of pregnant workers; no workers' compensation;

meager factory health care facilities; and tightly monitored bathroom breaks (ILRF 2007). Wal-Mart's supply factories frequently lock their exits in order to keep workers from stealing, a practice which has led to both fires and deaths. Anita Chan and Jonathan Unger (2011) claim that "when Wal-Mart brags of 'everyday low prices,' it is these workers that ultimately pay the price" (A16).

Wal-Mart's claim that their Ethical Standards Program prevents such abuses ignores what Lichtenstein sees as "an absolute conflict between Wal-Mart's drive for low prices and its effort to enforce a code of conduct" (2009, 227; Chan and Unger 2011). Critics argue that Wal-Mart deliberately and cynically obscures this conflict through relying on subcontractors, a weak inspection system, and a shift away from branded products. Wal-Mart's system of sub-contractors is dense, multi-layered, and difficult to regulate or inspect, allowing both the company and its consumers to effectively distance themselves from these "global" abuses. These unlicensed second- and third-tier contractors, however, are among the most exploitative in the business. Although Wal-Mart established a guideline and inspection system in the wake of the child labor scandal in 1992, compliance is voluntary and therefore weak, rendering its effect on manufacturing more symbolic than real. Fishman (2005) concludes that there are too few inspectors to even begin regulating existing factories, and that the program is dramatically underfunded. Moreover, factory owners are typically warned prior to inspections, and bosses routinely coach employees about how to lie to inspectors about conditions and wages.

Workers at many points in the global supply chain strike to protest inhumane conditions, but the consequences can be grave. Journalist Kari Lydersen (2011) reports that although uprisings occur "every few days in recent years," the participants remain vulnerable to injury and even death. The story of Bangladeshi labor activist and former sweatshop employee Kalpona Akter dramatically illustrates this point.[42] Akter faces either life in prison or the death penalty for organizing workers at a Wal-Mart subcontractor in Bangladesh to raise the minimum wage in a Wal-Mart subcontracted factory to a meager $71 per month.[43] Akter attended the 2011 ASM in Fayetteville and read a shareholder proposal—which was ultimately voted down—asking Wal-Mart to "tell their vendor to drop the charges." Activists like Akter demand that Wal-Mart acknowledge their relationship to these abusive factories, and intervene to protect workers. They ask all of us to cease accepting that "this is just how the world works," and to instead imagine and create a supply chain that does not depend on human suffering and exploitation.[44]

Unfortunately, abuses in "sweatshop" factories—the lived effects of "squeez-ing" low costs from vendors—are all too common. But workers are human beings, whose bodies and biological needs present limits to an infinite squeeze. Journalist David Moberg discussed these limits with the manager of an apparel

Figure 7.1 Members of the Bangladeshi National Garment Workers Federation strike for a higher minimum wage. Photo by the National Garment Workers Federation. Used with permission.

factory in Bangladesh, who explained that, "Expectations on quality are up, also on managing logistics. The lead time is squeezed. Getting fabric is difficult. Everything is getting squeezed." The unsustainability of the "squeeze" was made clear to him when he realized that his workers "[could no]t survive" on the government-stipulated minimum wage of $42 per month but that paying them a higher wage—he claimed to pay them $90—risked his relationship with Wal-Mart. The manager hoped that improved infrastructure in the village would provide workers with basics like water and electricity, allowing him to cut back on the wages. Moberg, asked: "Would[n't] Wal-Mart one day just move some place cheaper?" The manager responded, "Where will they move?"

Where indeed? Low standards for workers' rights have become normalized throughout the globe. These deplorable conditions remain invisible to most "first world" consumers, who often proceed as if they did not exist. Many who recognize and disagree with these realities do not see an alternative, in part because the causes of global asymmetries remain mystified. Wal-Mart's narrative of globalization perpetuates this ignorance.

Reframing Exploitation as Benevolence

In Wal-Mart's estimation, their global labor sourcing, although problematic, is both improving and preferable to the alternatives for many of their supply chain workers; indeed, Wal-Mart promotes offshore manufacturing as a path to economic advancement. This has been demonstrated most recently by the company's world hunger initiative [www.walmartstores.com/pressroom/news/10395.aspx], whose goal is to source $1 billion worth of agricultural products by 2015 from small farmers using sustainable methods. This represents just one of a cluster of programs designed to help small and medium farmers—half of whom they claim will be women—become sustainable producers and gain access to markets.[45] But labor rights activists question the notion that low-wage manufacturing jobs lead to economic advancement. The International Labor Rights Forum (ILRF) [www.laborrights.org/] contends that sweatshop employment needlessly endangers millions, offers little room for advancement, and robs workers of their futures.[46]

Scholars and labor rights advocates have been critical of the deliberately oversimplified way that multinational corporations like Wal-Mart frame the issues of globalization and development. Wal-Mart routinely ignores its own integral role as one of the largest and most powerful agents of asymmetrical globalization. Wal-Mart downplays the considerable leverage that they have with the governments of countries from whom they source; governments who hope to keep Wal-Mart's dollars flowing understand the economic disadvantage they would incur were they to more forcefully regulate wage scales or factory conditions. The implicit threat that the company might go elsewhere in search of lower costs is made possible—and given teeth—by the neoliberal regulatory framework that allows for the free movement of capital. Countries hampered by colonial histories, violence, and asymmetrically-structured debt regimes are increasingly vulnerable to such threats, and therefore more likely to keep this abusive and harmful system in place. Wal-Mart's rhetoric also ignores the actions of other companies, including Nike and Reebok, who have improved workplace conditions in order to protect their brand reputation.

Erasing (Post)colonial History

A critical omission in Wal-Mart's representation of global poverty regards how so-called "third world" countries became poor in the first place, or of the mechanisms through which this unequal world has been maintained. It ignores centuries of colonialism and imperial domination [http://qed.princeton.edu/index.php/User:Student/European_Colonialism_1500_AD_to_2000], through which the economies of North America and Europe were fortified at the expense of Latin America, China, Africa, and Southern Asia. Colonial rule involved the disruption of local subsistence practices, the capturing of peasantries and sequestration of their land for commodity agricultural production, the plundering of natural resources, and the destruction and hindrance of local industries (Wolf 1982; Escobar 1995). These processes began with the violent defeat and disestablishment of indigenous forms of governance, and were maintained by a military apparatus. After bloody independence struggles, postcolonial nations faced many problems, including ethnic divisions and poverty.

Wal-Mart's representation also omits the role of western models of development, and most recently neoliberalism, in maintaining poverty and global asymmetry, and the coercive means through which these models were imposed (Escobar 1995). Struggling to emulate the western path to industrial development, many countries in the global south undertook massive loans from the International Monetary Fund [www.imf.org/external/] and the World Bank [www.worldbank.org/]. As yet, most have been unable to replicate the economic success of Northern Europe and the U.S.; this is partly because these countries did not have other regions to colonize. Many became saddled with debt, and when higher interest payments led to inflation and crisis in the 1980s, the IMF offered to refinance their debt on the condition that they undertake neoliberal economic reforms, including: cutting government spending on public services; privatizing state services; and opening markets to foreign investment. Governments went along with these programs usually because they had little choice, and often against the will of their populations, whose opposition was frequently repressed.

Many critics see neoliberalism as a failure, especially for the postcolonial world, where it has led to higher rates of poverty and inequality (Stiglitz 2002; Harvey 2007). Austerity has created vast numbers of abandoned citizens who encounter their governments primarily as an oppressive force. Market openness has flooded domestic markets with subsidized crops from U.S. multinational oligopolies like Monsanto, which undermine agricultural production, a problem compounded by reduced governmental investment. Working classes around the world compete with one another to provide the lowest wages possible to attract foreign investment. Rising unemployment has fostered the growth of giant urban slums (Davis 2006), and driven waves of economic migrants into Europe and the U.S. Resource extraction has displaced populations, caused untold environmental devastation, and fueled seemingly intractable conflicts while the profits go elsewhere, a pattern that economists call the "resource curse" [www.oxfam.org/en/policy/lifting-resource-curse]. Instead of recognizing how neoliberalism contributes to poverty and asymmetry, Wal-Mart presents free markets as the solution to these problems. It is through reinforcing this dangerously misleading conceptual backdrop—devoid of history, power, and politics—that Wal-Mart strives to present itself as a neutral force trying to "help" or make a difference.

Wal-Mart and Global Retail

Foreign expansion plays a central role in the marketing strategies of the "Next Generation Wal-Mart," which emphasize the company's cosmopolitan and multicultural personality. At the 2011 ASM, for example, we met a film crew hired by Wal-Mart to document the company's international associates as they de-boarded buses onto the Bentonville town square and piled into the Visitor Center housed in Sam Walton's first Five and Dime. Having been bused directly from the airport, and donning brightly colored t-shirts marking countries of origin from South Africa to Chile, these visitors resembled pilgrims more than tourists as they honored the homeland of their multinational employer.

Launched in 1991 with a single discount store in Mexico City, Wal-Mart's international division now has stores in 26 countries, and accounts for

Figure 7.2 Filming associates in Bentonville during the 2011 ASM.

25 percent of their business. In each new locale, Wal-Mart has had to engage in a process of translation between their own corporate culture and local customs and tastes, including negotiating with unions (Mui 2011). Thus far the company has experienced mixed results, often succeeding, sometimes failing, and frequently encountering significant opposition. Though Wal-Mart has developed an array of persuasive tactics to facilitate their entry into these new markets, allegations of bribery in Mexico, made by *The New York Times* in 2012, have heightened suspicion toward the company, at least temporarily.

After entering Mexico, Wal-Mart moved north to Canada, where they aggressively negotiated the country's union-friendly climate by closing a unionized store (in Jonquière, Quebec). Soon thereafter, the company acquired ASDA, an existing chain in the United Kingdom that was modeled on Wal-Mart and already popular. ASDA grew stronger with the infusion of capital from Bentonville, though Wal-Mart's UK growth was briefly stymied by zoning laws and a strong union affiliated with ASDA's warehouse workers (these workers became the first to successfully organize under Wal-Mart's ownership). These early successes were followed by an utter failure in Germany, where the company's business model ran up against planning and zoning regulations, a strong union culture, and national "fair trading" regulations designed to protect local competition (Knorr and Arndt 2003; Meyerson 2011). In addition, German employees and shoppers actively disliked the company's culture, leading to poor sales and an even worse public image.

Wal-Mart has slowly expanded its retail presence in China, where their nearly 200 stores cater to affluent urban consumers (Chan and Unger 2011). Their limited success is owed, in part, to the company's willingness to adapt, like allowing the store to more closely resemble traditional Chinese markets [www.buzzfeed.com/mjs538/16-products-they-only-sell-at-chinese-walmarts] and negotiating with the state run union. Wal-Mart was relieved to discover that unlike unions in the U.S., the All-China Federation of Trade Unions was subservient to management (Lichtenstein 2009; Chan and Unger 2011). Wal-Mart gained a foothold across Africa in 2011 when it acquired a majority share of the South Africa-based retail chain Massmart, which operates in 12 African countries. A court ruled that the deal required concessions to African unions, however, which could complicate the retailer's plans for the region.

The rest of this chapter will focus on two foreign markets: India, where Wal-Mart is currently fighting to gain access, and Mexico, where Wal-Mart has carried out its longest-running and, until recently, most successful expansion. In both countries, Wal-Mart is a flashpoint for high stakes debates about the possibilities and risks of neoliberal economic frameworks.

The Global Direct Farm Program: The Solution for India?

With nearly one billion people, a growing urban middle class, and $400 billion in potential sales, Wal-Mart is working hard to gain access to India's retail market, where laws currently limit Foreign Direct Investment (FDI) in retail. In 2007, Wal-Mart began a very limited joint venture with the Bhatri group; they are currently permitted to sell to wholesalers and business owners, but not directly to the public. Wal-Mart has framed their entry as a solution for two problems confronting the Indian food system: food price inflation coupled with low prices for struggling farmers (Denyer 2011).

Although India had the first grain surplus in years in 2011–2012, much was wasted while 250 million people were undernourished (Bajaj 2012). The Public Distribution System (PDS) is run at an enormous loss, and critics say it is inefficient and corrupt. The situation has sparked calls to modernize and privatize. *The Economist* (2011) described India's retail industry as "primitive and wasteful," and a "glaring example of the need for foreign investment." India's ruling party, the United Progressive Alliance (UPA), agrees, and sees Wal-Mart as the answer. As part of its sustainability initiative, Wal-Mart announced a Global Direct Farm Program that aims to "support small-and medium-sized farmers and their communities," educating them about "seed and crop quality, soil use, and more."[47] Wal-Mart further claims that "by selling directly to Wal-Mart and eliminating the middleman, farmers earn a better price for their products, increase their incomes and receive expert advice on crop planning." In this way, Wal-Mart portrays itself as a development agency with the solution to India's food crisis. In a visit with President Barack Obama in 2010, Prime Minister Manmohan Singh echoed the company's rhetoric, saying that Wal-Mart's entry into the Indian market "could enable farmers to get higher prices and consumers to have to pay less" by eliminating "middle men" and extending the life of perishable foods through refrigeration (Denyer 2011). On the strength of these arguments, Wal-Mart is expected to be approved in 2012.

But Indians fighting against the retailer question this construction of the problem as well as the desirability of Wal-Mart's solution. Small store owners and street vendors, for example, see their livelihoods threatened by the "airtight" logic of efficiency. The neighborhood stores known as *kirana* that currently control India's grocery market and employ millions of people would have difficulty competing with Wal-Mart, whose elimination of the middlemen would cause massive unemployment. One of India's leading environmental activists, Vandana Shiva (2007), predicts disaster for India's small businesses:

India is a huge, huge land of bazaars, of huts, of markets. Every street is a market. Hawkers come down in the morning, get us our vegetables to

Figure 7.3 Neighborhood market located in the Safdar Jung development area in south
          Delhi. Photo by Ayesha Sood. Used with permission.

our doorstep. Of course, that's not very good for Wal-Mart so they're
manipulating zoning laws, shutting down hawkers, shutting down businesses in town, so that we will have a Wal-Mart model. But that means
100 million people out of retail and we don't know how much more
carbon emissions, while Wal-Mart talks about going green.

Furthermore, in Shiva's view, India's disorganized retail sector already achieves
near, if not direct, connections between growers and consumers, and is a
centerpiece of India's democratic political culture (Shiva 2006).

Wal-Mart's framing also ignores the history of the current food problem
and the plight of small farmers. Farming is the largest sector of the Indian
economy, employing over 250 million people. Most farmers have very small
plots and depend heavily on costly chemicals and pesticides that have
deteriorated land output. Many farm only for subsistence. Most critics link the
current food crisis to the flood of cheap imports from the U.S. after the market
opening in the early 1990s. Market liberalization allowed U.S. corporations
like Monsanto and Cargill to dump highly subsidized crops like wheat on the
Indian market, thus undercutting Indian production. Monsanto was also allowed
to introduce patented, genetically modified seeds that are illegal to save
[hwww.wired.com/science/discoveries/news/2005/01/66282].

Following neoliberal precepts, the Indian government cut subsidies, credit, and extension services for rural farmers, even as the cost of chemical inputs has risen. Critics fault this "dishonest" trade system for a crisis that has led tens of thousands of desperate farmers to commit suicide (Sainath 2011). Meanwhile, rapid urbanization, driven by the rural crisis and government policy, gobbled up agricultural land, and market speculation led to food price inflation. The recent renewal of government subsidies to farmers spurred an increase in production, but food prices remain high; the PDS, long neglected by budget cuts, often does not reach the poor, who rely on these subsidized grains. Journalist and activist Palagummi Sainath (2010) blames hunger on "the corporate hijacking of farming and the wrong . . . policies," that have created a situation in which "the farmers have no control over seeds, pesticides, fertilizers, power, water or the prices." Wal-Mart would not address these problems, which were produced by neoliberal policies, and their small farmer training would most likely accelerate the trend toward patented seeds and chemical agriculture.

Furthermore, it is not clear why Wal-Mart's tight supply chain would increase access to food for the rural poor—most of who could neither access nor afford to shop at Wal-Mart—or how it will lead to higher prices for small producers. Indeed, in India, the main supporters of FDI in retail are industrial food processing interests who want to be the players in Wal-Mart's supply chain (Goswami 2012). They have already pushed state policy away from credit for small farmers in favor of subsidies for industrial food cultivation, processing, and storage systems geared for urban consumption. Industrial processors want to purchase directly from small farmers and then sell to Wal-Mart, who would in turn bring lower food prices to the urban middle class, bypassing the poor. Even these Indian processors might soon be replaced by the retailer in its quest for efficiency (Sainath 2011).

In the name of providing food security to Indian farmers, Wal-Mart would further consolidate the shift in development priorities toward high tech industrial production geared toward the needs of the growing urban middle classes, at great risk to the food security of 830 million rural Indians (Goswami 2012). It bears repeating the conclusion of Nobel Prize winning economist Amartya Sen (2001), that famine in India has less to do with the *quantity* of food and more to do with the politics of its distribution. The roots of India's food crisis go much deeper than the solution proposed by Wal-Mart, which poses unique risks to food security. Wal-Mart's objective, after all, is not to feed India's poor, but to turn a profit.

Wal-Mart de Mexico: Shining Success or Foreign Invasion?

As the first and most successful foreign expansion effort, Wal-Mart de Mexico has served as a cherished sign of the company's ideal future and the universality and preeminence of their business model. Wal-Mart de Mexico's growth was initially facilitated by a joint venture with an existing chain named Cifra and the merged company eventually became the basis for Sam's Clubs in Mexico (Chavez 2002; Tilly 2006). With the help of the North American Free Trade Agreement (NAFTA) (Juhasz 2005), and an aggressive—possibly illegal—expansion strategy, Wal-Mart developed 2,088 stores under several different names, in addition to several chain restaurants. Mexico accounts for nearly half of Wal-Mart's total foreign retail operations [www.walmartstores.com/AboutUs/277.aspx?p=246], and approximately 20 percent of Wal-Mart stores are in Mexico. By 2003, Wal-Mart controlled over half of Mexico's retail market, and became the country's largest private employer (Chavez 2002). This success story, however, might literally be too good to be true, representing instead a set of illegal and often harmful practices associated with aggressive multinational expansion.

Wal-Mart's expansion into Mexico was aided by NAFTA, which was ratified in 1994, and both Wal-Mart and NAFTA were opposed by many of the same groups: domestic retailers, unions, farmers, and a host of "ordinary" Mexicans, many of who became involved in "site fights" similar to those in the U.S. A major one of these was sparked by Wal-Mart's decision to open a store near Teotihuacan [http://whc.unesco.org/en/list/414/], the 2,000-year-old UNESCO World Heritage site located 30 miles north of Mexico City that is home to the pyramids of the sun and moon (Ross 2005; Walker et al. 2006). Teotihuacan is sacred for many Mexicans as part of the country's indigenous history and identity, leading figures like Miguel Limon-Portillo, an acclaimed specialist in Aztec poetry, to furiously remark: "Wal-Mart has profaned the City of the Gods and there are no deities in Meso-America that can protect it now" (Ross 2005). That store opened amid protests in 2004, leaving a cloud of acrimony and enshrining a widespread perception of Wal-Mart as a "foreign invasion"—an embodiment of the threat to Mexican sovereignty and economic security made possible by NAFTA and a political lightning rod.

Tensions around the store erupted again in May, 2006, when flower vendors set up shop on the proposed site of another Wal-Mart near Teotihuacan, this one on the site of the Texcoco local market. When blocked by police, some vendors resisted, and were beaten and arrested. They sought help from residents in the nearby town of San Salvador Atenco, who had blocked the construction of a new airport on their land in 2002 and had since joined the Zapatista's "Other Campaign," which sought to organize poor and marginalized

Figure 7.4 Members of the Dry River Collective in Tucson make signs to protest the
violence in Atenco, Mexico. Photo by the Dry River Collective. Used with
permission.

groups across the country. The Zapatistas [http://lanic.utexas.edu/project/
Zapatistas/] are indigenous people from Chiapas Mexico who led a rebellion
against NAFTA on January 1, 1994, which they saw as a direct attack on their
communities. The Zapatistas organized the Other Campaign in 2006, in opposition to the existing political system, which they perceived as "sold out" to
foreign corporations. The vendors also sought assistance with the Popular Front
in Defense of Land, another Zapatista-aligned group.

Residents of Atenco protested armed with machetes and sticks. Mexican
President Enrique Peña Nieto, then the Governor of the state of Mexico,
ordered a brutal police crackdown that involved hundreds of arrests, dozens
of reported cases of sexual assault, and the murder of two people (Thomas
2006; Amnesty International 2007). Several police officers were also assaulted
and 16 activists are serving life sentences. State violence facilitated Wal-Mart's
expansion in Texcoco against public opposition. Zapatista spokesman, Subcommandante Marcos condemned the violence and demanded the prisoners'
release.[48]

Opposition to Wal-Mart is well-founded. As in the U.S., Wal-Mart puts "continuous pressure" on vendors to both improve their products and "force them to accept relatively low prices" (Iacovone et al. 2011), or "exit [the market] entirely" (Javorcik et al. 2008, 2). Suppliers also adopted efficiency measures that lowered wages throughout the supply chain (Juhasz 2005; Durand 2007). The entry of multinational retailers into Mexico spurred supply chain consolidation that excluded small farmers (Schwentesius and Gomez 2002) and, contrary to local sourcing rhetoric, NAFTA rules allowed Wal-Mart to cause a "tremendous" increase in imports (Durand 2007). In fact, Wal-Mart's purchases from small farmers account for a very small percentage of their total sales in Mexico.[49] These factors gave Wal-Mart an edge over local competitors.

As with Indian market liberalization, NAFTA precipitated a food crisis by opening the door to cheap agricultural imports, displacing local producers, and causing widespread unemployment and immigration (Bello 2008; Ross 2008). Mexico, where humans first domesticated corn, now imports corn from the U.S. Thousands of Wal-Marts have not solved this crisis, and their imports and supplier squeeze have instead likely contributed to it. Wal-Mart remains out of reach for the impoverished majorities who work and shop in the informal economy (Tilly 2006).

Tilly concludes that "there may be reasons to fear negative impacts of Wal-Mart's explosive growth in Mexico, but most of these reasons appear to apply with equal force in the rest of the retail sector" (2006, 190), much of which had already modeled itself, to a significant extent, after Wal-Mart. Bribery, however, may very well have created an unfair advantage for Wal-Mart; indeed, former Wal-Mart de Mexico executive Sergio Cicero Zapata, who blew the whistle on corruption allegedly overseen by Chief Executive Eduardo Castro Wright, told the *New York Times* that this was the entire point:

> [Mr. Castro-Wright's] idea . . . was to build hundreds of new stores so fast that competitors would not have time to react. Bribes, he explained, accelerated growth. They got zoning maps changed. They made environmental objections vanish. Permits that typically took months to process magically materialized in days. "What we were buying was time," he said.
>
> (Barstow 2012)

In 2005, there were a total of 326 Wal-Mart stores (Tilly 2006, 196), there were 722 by 2012. This kind of illegal hyper expansion devastated competitors and probably tightened Wal-Mart's grip on the supply chain, consolidating their advantage into the future.

The bribery scandal might affect Wal-Mart's ability to maintain their Mexican presence and to enter new markets. It has already tarnished Wal-Mart's image in India (Swamy 2012). Further scrutiny of the impacts of Wal-Mart's expansion on the Mexican food supply chain might make it more difficult for Wal-Mart to present itself as a safer option than an overhaul of the PDS, the path preferred by reformist groups in India.

Alternatives to Asymmetrical Globalization

Labor rights advocates and anti-globalization activists insist that Wal-Mart's exploitative model of globalization is neither just nor inevitable. Activist Kalpona Akter uses the language of human rights to encourage Wal-Mart to invest in Bangladesh in an ethical way.[50] Organizations like The ILRF and Sweatfree Communities [www.sweatfree.org/] fight to establish a stronger regime of international workers' rights and a universal living wage. They argue that Wal-Mart is uniquely positioned to establish a real set of standards, independently monitored and enforced, that would ensure just and humane working conditions.

Many activists also propose a form of development that begins with addressing the historical inequalities between and within countries, and oppose the mechanisms through which they are maintained in the present. The Jubilee Debt Campaign [www.jubileedebtcampaign.org.uk/], for example, calls for the forgiveness of foreign debt that keeps poor countries subordinate to Europe and the U.S. Economists Joseph Stiglitz and Andrew Charlton (2005) advocate providing foreign farmers and traders better access to international markets by eliminating subsidies and tariffs that unfairly benefit developed countries. Local activists like Shiva and Sainath propose that a shift to sustainable organic subsistence agriculture based in local knowledge would be more effective in both the short- and the long-terms.

Such solutions require us to think outside the logic of free markets. Paul Farmer [www.pih.org/] (2004) calls for addressing staggering inequalities in the global economy that cause structural violence, i.e., unnecessary social suffering borne primarily by the poor. He writes that "as a physician who has worked for much of my adult life among the poor of Haiti and the United states, I know that the law of supply and demand will rarely serve the interests of my patients" (2004, 5). Discussions of new economic frameworks are certainly warranted when over a billion of the world's people live in extreme poverty, and are unable to secure basic provisions, despite years of promises that free markets would make them available.

Although Wal-Mart insists it is compatible with all the cultures of the world, its dream of global coverage is part of the culture of neoliberal capitalism, which many groups view as fundamentally incompatible with their values as well as their well-being. The Zapatistas are one such group. They see neoliberalism as tantamount to a war on poor people worldwide, people who have little economic value, who benefit little from "free trade," and whose ways of life are "in the way" of resource extraction (Marcos 2001). After their initial uprising in 1994, the Zapatistas laid down their weapons, and began constructing an autonomous government against a vicious campaign of military repression. They worked nationally to organize and publicize the plight of groups whose voices are excluded in the current political system.

Instead of a world where money determines value, the Zapatistas assert the intrinsic dignity of poor indigenous communities and their rights to land and resources. Instead of making all cultures of the world compatible on one overarching plane of value, a fair description of Wal-Mart's aims, they dream of a world free from market logic, "a world in which many worlds are possible." While often seen as unrealistic idealists, the Zapatistas' message resonates widely among Mexicans, as well as with anti-globalization activists worldwide.

8

WAL-MART AND
FREEDOM

In 1992, shortly before Sam Walton's death, President George Herbert Walker Bush awarded him the Congressional Medal of Freedom, the nation's highest civilian honor. Upon his death, Walton was the richest person in America. Bush's award letter characterized Walton in the following terms: "An American original, Sam Walton embodies the entrepreneurial spirit and epitomizes the American Dream." Through the iconic figure of Sam Walton, President Bush defined American freedom as synonymous with free market capitalism.

Freedom is the central value in American society, encompassing the ability to worship, think, associate, travel, own weapons, elect leaders through a democratic process, and pursue wealth and property. Most Americans see these as inalienable rights and freedom as a universal value. Freedom is understood to be synonymous with the collective good: most Americans believe that the government exists to protect, preserve, and maximize freedom for the nation. American foreign policy is conducted in the name of bringing freedom and democracy to the world, and it is what U.S. soldiers die to protect.

Americans recognize that our freedom has limits when it harms the freedom of others; we surrender certain freedoms in order to protect the collective good. But the question of how to best safeguard freedom is complicated by conflicting definitions of freedom and of the collective good. For example, Americans disagree about the type of arms that individuals should be able to bear, as well as about the government's role in restricting their ownership. Some gun control advocates think the constitutional right to bear arms does not extend to automatic weapons. Their freedom to live in a society with fewer guns is legally subordinated to the freedom of those who want to own them.

Freedom is typically understood as a negative state—the absence of a coercive power telling us what to do, think, or endure. Americans see the pursuit of individual self-interest on the free market as the epitome of freedom, of true human nature in the absence of governmental constraint. Through this framework, we see market economies as pure expressions of human freedom to choose, rather than as actively constructed by governmental intervention and enforced through police mechanisms. The history of modern liberal societies reveals a more complicated picture of a "double edged character [to] freedom" that is often overlooked (Rose 1999, 67). Even in *laissez faire* capitalism, freedom exists only *under certain conditions* that are shaped by the government, a non-market force. In nineteenth-century Britain, governments passed vagrancy laws, built prisons, and fenced off the commons in order to create a workforce for new factories. Workers were "freed" from their subsistence practices—now deemed illegal—to seek wage labor. At the same time that the government violently engineered the "free" labor market, they banned group organization, helping to ensure a docile workforce that was then subject to further regulation and discipline in the factories (Rose 1999, 70).

Similarly, the cotton plantation economy in the American South was built through both the forced removal of Native Americans and the slave trade, and the violent disruption of subsistence practices to conquer a labor force happened throughout the colonized world. All of these economies depended on the subordination of women and the exploitation of their (typically unpaid) labor. These histories demonstrate how governments actively construct and reinforce economic systems by giving legal backing to forms of domination that exclude alternative models. Modern liberal freedom was founded on many forms of *unfreedom* that we collectively and conveniently forget.

Americans rarely question the limits of the political fields that we both occupy and play a role in producing, if only by accepting the experiences of freedom that they render normal and inevitable. Anthropologists examine and compare specific visions and lived experiences of freedom, and explore their boundaries, constraints, and contradictions. We also examine how certain models of freedom become normalized, habituated, and taken for granted, while others are repressed or rendered invisible. This book has attempted to further the anthropology of American freedom in the current political economic order by examining the lived experiences of people both inside of and connected to the world's largest and most influential corporation.

Wal-Mart's Vision of Freedom and Rights

Wal-Mart enacts a particular conception of freedom in the way that they diagnose the failure of the American Dream, and in the treatment they propose. Wal-Mart's reconfiguration of the Dream enshrines a market-centric definition of freedom and human rights that subordinates collective material rights to the rights of individuals to accumulate wealth. As they attempt to morph into the "Next Generation Wal-Mart" in order to appeal to people in cosmopolitan urban areas and in impoverished regions around the globe, they increasingly present themselves as the solution to liberal causes like equality, environmental protection, and food security. They present these ambitious goals as entirely consistent with their prime objective of generating profits for shareholders, and with a global economy based on individual and international competition and perpetual economic growth.

Beyond Sam Walton's considerable business skills, Wal-Mart's success is rooted in a profound failure of our society and our prevailing political and economic systems to include everyone in the American Dream. These exclusions are a living legacy of our shared histories of discrimination and exploitation, made increasingly visible and acute through our decades-long embrace of free market policies. In this world of exclusion, poverty, and unrealized aspirations, Wal-Mart appears to many people as a revolutionary step toward freedom.

One significant "Wal-Mart effect" is that it has made life in the harsh and unequal economy more livable for millions. However, Wal-Mart does not solve poverty, social inequality, or environmental destruction. While it may ameliorate these harms in certain ways, it exacerbates them in others, often outweighing any positive effects. Another hidden consequence of Wal-Mart's "solution" is the strengthening and normalizing of the structures and policies that created the social problems that it purports to solve.

As Wal-Mart has delivered on specific experiences of freedom, it has exercised its own. Legally, and like any other corporation, Wal-Mart is considered a person [www.npr.org/2011/10/24/141663195/what-is-the-basis-for-corporate-personhood], yet one with more rights and less accountability than any individual (Ehrenreich 2011a). Wal-Mart exercises its freedom to grow while maximizing shareholder profits, often even breaking the law. Wal-Mart exercises its freedom to hire and manage their employees as they see fit. It exercises its right to censor products that gesture toward political dissent or transgress certain norms of decency. It exercises its free speech in the store, in their anti-union campaigns, and in the public sphere where it purchases unimaginable hours of commercial time and advertising space and helps fund political campaigns. Wal-Mart promises it will bring the best possible outcomes of happiness and fulfillment to consumers, employees, producers, the nation, the environment—and indeed, the world. They simultaneously fight for their right to conduct business in an unimpeded manner: to squeeze a global chain of suppliers and subcontractors; to sprawl; to pollute; to source their products, albeit indirectly, from the hands of children and other near-slaves; to pay low wages; to union-bust; and to avoid responsibility for systematic discrimination.

Anthropologists Peter Benson and Stuart Kirsh (2010) use the phrase "harm industries" to describe industries that entail inevitable human costs, like mining and tobacco production. Extending this logic, Wal-Mart is a central nexus in the "harm economy" of neoliberal capitalism, as it thrives on offering partial and deeply flawed solutions to its exclusions and failures while working to provide aesthetic and ethical justification for an economic system that is fundamentally hostile to human beings and nature. Wal-Mart's business model and cultural politics do more than simply defend and grow the store, they normalize and reinforce neoliberal capitalism itself.

More than anything else, Wal-Mart's vision of freedom focuses on the experience of the individual shopper, whose freedom they claim to maximize through low prices, wide selection, convenience, and friendly service. These low prices, which, as the company reminds us, save the average family some $3,100 annually, are significant in an era of economic stagnation and rising costs. But the immediate, tangible experience of consumer freedom trades off with other things that many of us think are equally, if not more, important (Dicker 2005). These tradeoffs result from the contradictory nature of the American Dream, especially the contradiction between the individual and the collective, or its private and public dimensions.

People are more than individual consumers: we are also workers, citizens, patriots, inhabitants of the natural environment, members of diverse communities, and practitioners of various faiths. We have multiple identities and we are members of collectives, whether we recognize this or not. Wal-Mart elevates the individual shopper aspect of our identities to the exclusion and detriment of our other dimensions, especially our collective ones. Wal-Mart's leveraging of information and purchasing power limits their suppliers' ability to set prices or to have humane and ethical working conditions. Their freedom to outsource manufacturing interferes with the freedom of working people to find well-compensated factory jobs; their ability to pay low wages and benefits runs counter to workers' desire to make a living wage and to have functioning social safety nets; Wal-Mart's slow and discriminatory promotion policies run counter to employees' freedom to move up the ladder to success; their freedom to demand hard, fast, and subservient work interferes with employees' desires for physical comfort and personal dignity; Wal-Mart's anti-union tactics undermine the freedom of employees to organize collectively and negotiate the terms of their labor; Wal-Mart's freedom to expand interferes with communities' desires to protect local businesses and preserve their local community character; Wal-Mart's freedom to sell in volume interferes with our freedom to enjoy an unpolluted and safe natural environment; and Wal-Mart's ability to influence politicians undermines citizens' freedom to have equal access to the government.

These trade-offs, unintended long-term consequences of our purchases, were at first difficult, if not impossible, to perceive; they happened slowly and out of sight. By the time they were widely recognized they were already entrenched in the ordinary. Little did we realize that something seemingly so wholesome, corny, and patriotic as Wal-Mart was steadily concentrating so much power and transforming our lives in such far-reaching ways, limiting and configuring the spaces and practices through which we exercise freedom. This invisibility was aided by the fact that Wal-Mart does everything in its considerable ability to present a positive, optimistic, and humble vision of the world that obscures these contradictions. With scandal and protests at every turn, Wal-Mart's image-crafters' hands are full. Their efforts, driven by the bottom line and not the public interest, have made it more difficult to have a meaningful dialogue about the real challenges facing our society and about a wider range of possible solutions, not just the ones Wal-Mart endorses.

The neoliberal definition of freedom espoused and promoted by Wal-Mart focuses our agency exclusively toward decisions we make between products, or in the ways in which we sell our labor in a highly competitive and very asymmetrical market. We have freedom to engage in individualized market activities understood as free individual choices. But our rights stop there. Wal-Mart's vision of freedom does not include rights to a minimum standard of material subsistence or workplace dignity, nor does it include a vision of social justice that strives to level the playing field. In their market-focused conception, human freedom is legitimately limited by unequal access to wealth, regardless of the non-market processes involved in its distribution. Although this is seen as acceptable because wealth is assumed to reflect individual effort and merit, economic class is profoundly influenced by race, gender, and national origin. In addition, Wal-Mart's vision of human rights does not recognize a collective right to be free of the negative effects of the market activities of other "free" individuals. Finally, Wal-Mart's vision of freedom specifically *excludes* the ability to act collectively in order to alter working conditions. Not only does Wal-Mart ignore the forms of structural violence identified by Paul Farmer and others, they vigorously work against our right to collectively remake the social structures and regulatory frameworks to address the variety of ways that structural violence limits our freedom. Although Wal-Mart claims to support basic political rights, as Farmer argues "civil rights cannot really be defended if social and economic rights are not" (Farmer 2004, 9).

Normalizing Wal-Mart's Definition of Freedom

Why do we accept Wal-Mart's market-centered vision of freedom? Wal-Mart insists that they are simply a product of employee and consumer choices, exercising their "right to work" and casting their "dollar votes" respectively. In an important sense, this is true: we animate Wal-Mart with our collective agency. And many of us love Wal-Mart for the access it gives us to the American Dream. But the company is anything but the product of a transparent democratic process. We did not in any simple way "choose" Wal-Mart; our choices are made under conditions that are often outside of our control. Just because we seek low prices or employment does not mean that we actively affirm everything sacrificed to obtain them, although some of us might. Yes, retailers respond to our changing purchasing patterns and labor market fluctuations. But these changes are always limited by the desire for profit maximization. Wal-Mart will change as needed if large numbers of people refuse to shop there for environmental or human rights reasons or if employees can find better paying jobs elsewhere. But individual shoppers have little knowledge about or control over the environmental and human conditions under which the products we purchase are produced, and individual laborers have little say over the market's demand for labor or the conditions under which they work. Even with environmental changes, core elements of the business model remain off the table: Wal-Mart has not budged, for example, on opposition to unionization in the U.S., universally low wages and benefits, monopsony control over producers, and the significant human rights concerns of their supply chain workers.

Journalist John Dicker (2005) sees a society addicted to low prices and unwilling to pay more for social responsibility. He hopes that "one day we'll have the courage to realize that our entitlement to 'cheap' is our new crack cocaine" (215). But many of us simply cannot afford to shop elsewhere. Others of us barely recollect how it all took shape, or connect the dots. We see low prices, not the externalities often borne by people and places out of our sight, or that affect us in ways we do not recognize. Many of the regulations favoring Wal-Mart have the advantage of being so taken for granted as to be nearly invisible; most even existed before Wal-Mart came along (Moberg 2011). Even if we do see the hidden costs, we can scarcely imagine an alternative to an order of things in which Wal-Mart plays a vital part of our everyday lives.

Wal-Mart's business model derives much of its legitimacy from the fact that most of us have internalized a limited neoliberal interpretation of freedom as the ultimate horizon of human possibility. This "normalcy" is not an accident, but a constant effort of many forces, including companies like Wal-Mart who have worked to enshrine their business model—and by extension the regulatory framework that supports it—as normal, beneficial, and outside the realm of political debate. For example, Bethany Moreton (2009) describes how Wal-Mart extolled a management philosophy of servant leadership that smoothed over contradictions between Christianity and capitalism.

Servant leadership is only one aspect in the larger constellation of Wal-Mart's hyper-simplified worldview in which the contradictions in the American

Dream, and the ways these have been exacerbated by neoliberalism, do not exist. They aggressively present a world studiously devoid of history and power in which the store exists as deeply ordinary—a non-problematic and apolitical entity. Cultural critic Lauren Berlant observes that "Central to ... national fantasy is a strong and enduring belief that the best of U.S. national subjectivity can be read in its childlike manifestations and in a polity that organizes its public sphere around a commitment to making a world that could sustain an idealized infantile citizen" (1997, 28). A historical timeline at the Wal-Mart Visitor Center is a prime example of this thinking: it describes the 1960s as "a time of revolutionary ideas, conflict, and savings." This frame evacuates both the content of the ideas and the stakes of the struggles, as well as any tension between the desire for radical social change and a life organized around market efficiency. Wal-Mart, the ultimate infantile citizen, appears as innocent, beneficial, and normal, as a gentle giant that replenishes our optimism for the American Dream, even as structural forces, among them Wal-Mart, increasingly block its realization.

Class inequalities are often naturalized by derogatory references to the race, gender, or national origin of those at the bottom of the social hierarchy. Wal-Mart, on the contrary, views social inequalities not as inevitable, but as capable of being resolved through shopping and working at Wal-Mart—ideal scenes of citizenship in "Wal-Mart country." However, rather than portraying American social hierarchies or international asymmetries as intrinsic to American society or the international world order, respectively—or as integral to their low wage business model—Wal-Mart presents these inequalities as minor aberrations that can be resolved through the approved mechanism of individual effort, either as a striving worker or an aspiring price-conscious shopper. Wal-Mart's response to the failure of the American Dream encourages us to invest individual agency into refashioning ourselves into more resilient subjects capable of surviving and competing in the free market, focusing on savings and self-improvement. Nikolas Rose observes how:

[i]t has become possible to actualize this notion of the actively respon-sible individual because of the development of new apparatuses that integrate subjects into a moral nexus of identifications and allegiances in the very processes in which they appear to act out their most personal choices.

(1996, 58)

Wal-Mart is one of the largest such apparatuses in the world. It markets itself to employees and shoppers as a "normative technology of citizenship that seeks to create proper subjects and subjectivities" (Berlant 1997, 31). Wal-Mart offers to help us become "entrepreneurs of ourselves" in a free market, an offer we experience as our own free will.

Yet another way that Wal-Mart's business model has become normalized is through selective concessions to their many critics. Since the mid-2000s, they have taken their case to the public, heavily advertising programmatic accommodations to environmentalism, diversity, equality, racial and women's empowerment, small businesses, and offering healthcare to their employees. Their philanthropic efforts often aim to counter criticisms on point. They present themselves as actively engaged in addressing every problem ever associated with their business model. They downplay the limited and selective nature of their solutions and their repeated failures to resolve the problems they address, while ignoring more direct structural solutions.

The failure of free market economic policies has exposed contradictions that lie at the heart of the American Dream. As these contradictions grew, Wal-Mart succeeded by using high efficiency logistics and exploiting a low wage workforce to manufacture a miniaturized version of the Dream that empowered vulnerable individuals to navigate an increasingly unequal and hostile socioeconomic terrain. In addition to fostering real experiences of belonging, saving, and self-improvement, as well as promoting a plausible and contradiction-free worldview, Wal-Mart deployed an effective anti-union strategy, and developed a sophisticated PR apparatus to deflect organized opposition or critique. They are now decades into the process of marketing their vision of consumer citizenship and the good life to the globe, and they have begun to explore new terrains, such as education and healthcare. Despite Wal-Mart's relentless attempts to justify their externalities in the name of low prices, defuse them through PR initiatives and partial accommodations, or erase them from popular consciousness altogether, the negative side effects of their business model continue to engender widespread ambivalence—a mix of repudiation, resignation, and attachment.

In an important sense, the political question becomes: who gets to define the ordinary? The neoliberal vision of freedom, along with its limitations, has become normal and acceptable for many of us, while Wal-Mart's place in our lives has become more habitual. Whether we love it or hate it, most of us take Wal-Mart's existence for granted, as if it had a life of its own, even as we actively produce it as a social fact. Even most of those who boycott the company and disagree with its politics accept a regulatory framework that allows it to exist in its current form. Benson and Kirsh (2010) suggest that the mining and tobacco industries' attempts to deflect criticisms contribute to apathy and political disengagement, what they call the "politics of resignation." Berlant asks whether "naïve infantile citizenship and paralyzed cynical apathy [are] the only positions a normal American can assume" (1997, 29). Many of us, even the critical minded, have abdicated our power to define the normal to corporations, even ones we do not like; we do not imagine that we or anyone else is capable of changing the situation.

Reimagining Freedom

Imagine an alien landed on earth and we asked them to find "freedom." Where would they look? Would they focus, as many of us do, on acts of consumption and the creation of private wealth? Would they look for the richest person in the world? What if instead they looked at everything that went into making that wealth possible? Would they see a happy child riding on a new bicycle from Wal-Mart as a pure expression of freedom? Or would they look at everything that went into creating that bicycle: the environmentally destructive extraction of the raw materials necessary for its construction; the grueling, fast-paced work in the factories machining and assembling the parts; the low wages and low benefits of the workers who ship and stock the bikes? Would the alien be able, as we often are, to separate process from the final product, erecting boundaries between types of people, stations in life, and citizens of different nations, and between humans and the natural environment? What might they think of our remarkable capacity to treat the deep complicities of our social systems with these unpleasant realities as if they did not exist? What do we think?

Many of Wal-Mart's critics promote alternative definitions of freedom that emerge from and exceed the limits of a market centered approach and that do not fall into paralyzed pessimism. While diverse, these critics challenge us to consider the benefits that Wal-Mart provides in light of the very real forms of suffering and unfreedom that Wal-Mart perpetuates. They warn that a regulatory system skewed to protect unrestricted freedom for massive corporations like Wal-Mart often means tyranny for everyone else. They call for balancing Wal-Mart's corporate freedom with the collective well-being of workers, communities, the nation, the environment, and the global community.

Rather than simply expressing gratitude for a job, labor unions and other workers challenge corporations like Wal-Mart by asking how free and in control of our lives we are when we do not have work that allows us to provide for our basic needs or that causes us physical harm (Ehrenreich 2011*b*). Furthermore, the Betty Dukes case, even in defeat, stands as a grim reminder of the way that Wal-Mart fought for retail dominance by systematically underpaying a primarily female and minority workforce (Featherstone 2005*a*). OUR Wal-Mart is further proof that employees' thirst for respect and forms of belonging are not limited by the corporate bottom line. Community activists and cultural preservationists urge Wal-Mart to respect the unique character and human significance of places. Some environmentalists criticize Wal-Mart's attempts to anesthetize our minds with optimism about their environmental efforts while diverting us from the hard choices that we need to make about our destructive consumption habits.

Anti-Wal-Mart activists and critics resonate with and parallel broader social movements and strands of critique that prescribe solutions to the failure of the Dream that go far beyond those marketed by Wal-Mart and other multinationals. In response to the current predicament, these groups confront the historical injustices and the contradictions between individual and collective at the heart of the Dream, and attempt to fashion new dreams that are truly sustainable, inclusive, and democratic. Unions and their allies urge a number of specific legal changes that would make it easier for employees to form a union, like the Employee Free Choice Act, as well as universal standards and protections for labor. In the U.S., the Rebuild the Dream [http://rebuildthe dream.com/] movement fights against fiscal austerity and in favor of significant public investment in poor and minority communities in order to overcome historical injustices. Like the civil rights movement, it defines patriotism in these terms. The Jubilee movement calls for forgiving the debt in formerly colonized countries as a beginning step to rectify the imbalances of the global economy. Indian activist Vandana Shiva [www.vandanashiva.org/] calls for sustainable agricultural solutions as a means of restoring food security, not "free trade" and the corporate control of the food supply that it represents. Environmentalists urge us to shift away from mass consumption to forms of subsistence more in harmony with the natural environment, both for its intrinsic value and for the survival of future generations. Some call for a more thorough rethinking of the ethics of a global economic system based on individual and interstate competition and the transformation of natural, social, and political capital into commodities that can be bought and sold. Zapatistas, for example, urge us to consider those groups that have no value in this system, and whose ways of life are being destroyed by the unchecked advance of capitalism. Still others call for decolonizing the world order through the creation of a global commons for vital resources—such as land, food, water, and energy—and for dismantling the structures of exploitative capitalism (Hardt and Negri 2000; Wallerstein 2004).[51] Farmer (2004), for example, calls for universal access to health care, and also for extending our conception of democracy outside of national boundaries.

These alternative visions of freedom do not calculate freedom solely in terms of private individual prerogatives and profits, but in terms of collective well-being. They seek balance between individual and collective needs and desires, and propose that these are not antithetical. They speak to the fundamentally shared nature of existence, the collective production of society, and the interdependence of individual and collective. These alternatives do not hold up citizenship as some sort of prize that has to be earned by as yet "unworthy" masses toiling in drudgery. They do not draw imaginary lines of compassion between citizens and non-citizens, racial groups, genders, humans, and nature. Instead, they extend our conception of human rights, labor rights, and environmentalism across borders, and enact dreams that are more inclusive, less hierarchical, more sustainable, and not exclusively "American."

Making Other Dreams Possible

Considering alternative perspectives on freedom urges us to think about the contemporary possibilities of collective action through which we could wrest control from powerful corporations and undemocratic political systems in order to put other dreams of freedom into motion. How can such a collective be achieved? Is it even possible? In *The Twilight of Equality*, cultural critic Lisa Duggan writes:

> In 1972 . . . I . . . had reason to be optimistic. Active and expanding social movements seemed capable of ameliorating conditions of injustice and inequality, poverty, war, and imperialism. In fact, social movements were producing innovative critiques of a widening variety of constraints on human possibility.
>
> (2003, 1)

Duggan further argues that these U.S. social movements were effectively compartmentalized and outmaneuvered during the transition to neoliberalism, which advanced on the heels of political appeals to racism, sexism, and sexual intolerance.

Popular democratic social movements aimed at addressing the fundamental contradictions in the late capitalist world order face serious obstacles. To begin with, current labor laws make certain forms of associational action—such as forming a union—either difficult or illegal, as is the case with sympathetic strikes and boycotts. These restrictions reflect the extent to which free market visions and notions of individual rights are legally codified. Furthermore, corporations have convinced many Americans that unions are a threat to employment and greedy and corrupt violators of individual rights. Conservatives paint free market policies and tax cuts as inextricably woven into the fabric of American life, and see regulation as a violation of sacrosanct ideals. They also criticize social spending in minority communities as disempowering handouts, and blame social inequalities on a lack of market discipline among poor minority communities.

Duggan argues that this trend can only be undone by forging alliances between the distinct groups—like economic immigrants and racial minorities —that have been marginalized by neoliberal policies, but whose politics are often seen as either unrelated or in conflict. What unites such groups, at least in part, is a desire for a regulatory framework based in notions of human rights and social justice rather than in market logic. Such similarities create opportunities for articulations between these movements, and make Wal-Mart a potential point against which these various movements can organize in mutual support.

Continued crises create new opportunity for social movements that question the political economic structures. The global economic recession prompted many Americans to question the free market progress narrative that insists on tax cuts, budget cuts, and deregulation at every turn. Many progressives hoped that the global economic meltdown of 2008 would stimulate a sustained national conversation about the limits and excesses of free market policies. Instead, anxiety over chronic unemployment and skyrocketing deficits created the conditions for the emergence of the Tea Party Patriots' movement, which called for a massively reduced role for government in social and economic life, reduced taxation and government spending, and for a return to the "original meaning" of the Constitution. Populists on the right blamed the nation's economic woes on "big government" and the deficit stimulus spending of the Obama administration.

Occupy Wall Street [http://occupywallst.org/] challenged the Tea Party's diagnosis of the problem and proposed solutions. Their critique of the "1 percent" placed inequality on the national agenda and blamed deregulation for the crisis, specifically rules that allowed banks to grow "too big to fail," posing systemic risks to the global economy. They echo the sentiment of progressives who are perplexed about how a radical recommitment to unrestricted free market capitalism and fiscal austerity emerged as the solution for an economic recession that they see as caused by these same policies. Among other demands, they advocate more restrictions on banking and corporate power.[52] Many analysts have wondered about the conditions under which this critique could catch on and become the basis for a sustained political movement with the power to challenge the order of things.

Numerous observers have expressed frustration with the ways that neoliberal thought has coopted mainstream political opposition in the U.S. and elsewhere, and with the seeming inability of collective agency or our current political systems to accomplish anything, much less create long-term meaningful change. Such feelings of resignation result from repressive political violence and governmental intransigence (Copeland 2011) as well as from corporations' ability to avoid ethical responsibility for the harms they cause (Benson and Kirsh 2010). Benson and Kirsh contend that an effective way to combat these feelings would be through a critique that emphasizes not only that some degree of harm is fundamental to specific industries but that the industries themselves are not inevitable (475). This observation applies to other sovereign entities, including nation-states and multinational corporations like Wal-Mart. However, recognizing the non-inevitable nature of certain harmful forms of capitalism or political organization is insufficient to dislodge the regulatory framework that produces and allows them to exist.

Forming a progressive alliance for the formation of an alternative global political order requires forging connections between the specific forms of identity-based subordination that neoliberalism has produced or exacerbated (Duggan 2004). Raw materials violently mined in the Congo become transformed into goods by exploited laborers in Bangladesh; they are then processed by harried immigrant warehouse workers in California and eventually stocked on shelves by poor, minority, and female workforces in the U.S. and the global retail sector. Critical to the formation of such a global alliance is a recognition that the distinct groups in this chain of human suffering share common interests—precisely what multinational corporations hope will not happen. Global capital is banking, quite literally, on the continued separation of these groups' struggles, both practically and in the popular imagination.

While Wal-Mart's critics do voice distinct concerns, the divisions between them are a product, to some extent, of the ways that they have been recognized and partially accommodated by the company as discrete and unrelated entities. Wendy Brown (1995) suggests that a key mechanism of neoliberal political systems for disabling organized opposition is to provide partial compensation for the injuries these systems inflict. Marginalized groups may become attached to their "wounded" identities and exchange a critique of the political system that excludes them for the benefits they receive as subordinates within it. Unlike neoliberal states, however, Wal-Mart rarely recognizes responsibility for harming workers in their supply chain, associates, or the communities where they want to expand. Rather, Wal-Mart provides forms of symbolic and affective inclusion for groups they are known to harm or exploit. Nevertheless, their efforts serve to maintain a separation between these affected groups and other constituencies.

Wal-Mart encourages shareholders to see themselves as individuals with private economic interests, and not as people who are concerned about discrimination, labor rights, or the environment. They attempt to woo African-Americans and Hispanics as poor minorities, and not as working people or as women. Environmental issues are dealt with as if they had no connection to human rights abuses, lowering wages, or racial exploitation. Environmentalists who now champion Wal-Mart's monopsony power forego a critique of the effects of that power on working people or American democracy. None of these groups are fully accommodated, because, beyond a certain level, their demands are incompatible with Wal-Mart's business model, which remains non-negotiable. This is one reason why Wal-Mart goes to great lengths to express gratitude to their associates and to make them feel like part of a family, but refuses to engage whatsoever with organized groups of employees.

Many opportunities exist for Wal-Mart's critics to cross lines of difference and provide mutual support and solidarity. Labor activists and community groups who oppose Wal-Mart's entry could focus their efforts toward providing sustainable alternatives to the food deserts that Wal-Mart claims to resolve in rural poor and urban minority communities. Workers themselves could come together across racial and gender divides to demand higher wages and better treatment. White, male, and straight workers could support the struggles of female, minority, and gay and lesbian workers against workplace discrimination. Minority communities eager to have Wal-Mart arrive could demand minimal protections and wages for workers in their stores. All of these groups could find common cause with immigrants who have been used by corporations to break unions and lower wages. Environmentalists could join forces with working people, and use their new position of inclusion in the company to fight for more radical transformations across the board, especially regarding labor conditions in the global supply chain, instead of seeing respect for nature and respect for human beings in two distinct categories. U.S. critics could unite with Wal-Mart's critics from foreign companies. Finally, those who maintain an ironic critical stance toward Wal-Mart could overcome their apathy and join the movements to change the company.

These efforts are already underway. Local coalitions, such as Respect DC [www.respectdc.org/] are negotiating Community Benefits Agreements in order to address the needs of multiple groups affected by Wal-Mart. OUR Wal-Mart is organizing working class associates across lines of gender and race in order to win more respect in the workplace. Warehouse Workers United are advocating not just for the rights of U.S.-based and vulnerable immigrants, but also for workers across the international supply chain. Finally, prominent activists like Terri O'Neill, the president of the National Organization for Women, see addressing labor rights issues at Wal-Mart, and inequality in general, as core feminist issues. Much more needs to be done along these lines to address these "intersectional identities," a task that feminists of color recognize as a crucial step in forming effective political alliances across diverse communities (Crenshaw 1991).

Figure 8.1 National Organization for Women President Terry O'Neill speaking at OUR
        Wal-Mart Protest in Bentonville. Photo by OUR Wal-Mart. Used with permission.

Alternative visions of freedom require reconfigured regulatory frameworks,
i.e., new cultural rules by which we organize economic and political life: how
we exploit the natural environment to meet human needs for survival;
how we assign property rights, mobilize labor, organize exchange, and distribute
surplus; and how we organize ourselves into groups and make political decisions
—in short, how we best govern ourselves. The possibilities for reconfiguration
are almost limitless, and anti-Wal-Mart movements provide numerous ideas of
places to start.

Anti-Wal-Mart movements could fruitfully extend beyond Wal-Mart and
examine the regulatory framework that enables the company to operate.
This would mean a direct confrontation with the market centric definition of
freedom. Wal-Mart's size and scope contain the potential to bring together
numerous groups frustrated with the conditions of life under neoliberalism.
This movement, and the concerns that it taps into, could cut across our traditional political categories. Unity among multiple groups opposed to neoliberal
economic policies was the spark of the social movements that toppled regimes
in Latin America over the last decade, as well as the Arab Spring movements
of 2011. Wal-Mart's permanent PR campaign on so many fronts reflects a
world order in a constant state of crisis management. Ultimately, Wal-Mart

may be forced to change by powerful citizen movements that would not only affect Wal-Mart, but reshape the ethical foundations of the global political economy.

The battle over Wal-Mart is a battle over the American Dream, which multinational corporations have helped make a global phenomenon. A question as important as how to reconfigure the Dream should not be decided by a powerful few to the exclusion of the many. It could and should be a democratic debate regarding the limits and possibilities of human freedom, and should include a wide range of ideas and perspectives. It could and should be framed in terms of the collective public interest, and not constrained by national boundaries. Those interested in these discussions should remember, that neoliberalism rose to dominance and outmaneuvered oppositional groups in large measure because of the hierarchical and exclusive nature of the social orders where it took root. Constructing lasting alternatives will require confronting tangled issues of social justice.

NOTES

1 Wal-Mart's Cultural Politics

1 www.vanityfair.com/magazine/2009/11/60-minutes-poll200911
2 http://people-press.org/2011/02/10/fewer-want-spending-to-grow-but-most-cuts-remain-unpopular
3 http://Wal-Martstores.com/AboutUs/295.aspx

2 From the Ozarks to the Planet

4 http://sprawl-busters.com/caseagainstsprawl.html
5 www.walmartstores.com/sites/ResponsibilityReport/2011/executive_summary.aspx
6 Duke, Mike "Sustainability Agriculture Remarks," October 14, 2010 http://walmartstores.com/pressroom/news/10394.aspx
7 hwww.shell.com/home/content/lubes/media_centre/news_media_releases/2011/bibendum_Wal-MartWalmart_honours_shell_lubricants.html

3 Wal-Mart Nation

8 http://Wal-Martstores.com/AboutUs/286.aspx
9 Ibid.
10 http://Wal-Martstores.com/pressroom/news/9550.aspx
11 http://rebuildthedream.com/

4 The People of Wal-Mart

12 http://Walmartstores.com/pressroom/news/10555.aspx
13 www.Wal-Martnyc.com, Community Journal (accessed June 1, 2011)
14 nyc.walmartcommunity.com
15 Ibid.
16 www.dressforsuccess.org/GoingPlaces.aspx
17 www.Wal-Martclass.com/all_faqs_index.html#a1
18 www.supremecourt.gov/opinions/10pdf/10-277.pdf
19 www.Wal-Martstores.com/Diversity/309.aspx
20 www.peopleofWal-Mart.com/
21 http://instoresnow.walmart.com/Community.aspx
22 Ibid.
23 www.aflcio.org/corporatewatch/Wal-Mart/Wal-Mart_2_profiles.cfm
24 www.reclaimdemocracy.org/Wal-Mart/minority_contractors.php
25 http://Wal-Martstores.com/pressroom/news/10555.aspx

5 Wal-Mart's Anti-Union Strategies

26 http://forrespect.org/our-Wal-Mart/about-us/
27 http://ourWal-Mart.org/trip-to-bentonville/
28 www.youtube.com/watch?v=3kzb1FMhxog (video coverage of rally)
29 www.unglobalcompact.org/AboutTheGC/TheTenPrinciples/principle3.html
30 Ibid.
31 www.youtube.com/watch?v=TynvVPTPuG0&feature=relmfu
32 www.warehouseworkersunited.org/
33 www.universallivingwage.org/
34 www.universallivingwage.org/; www.nationalhomeless.org/factsheets/who.html

6 The Space of Wal-Mart

35 www.sfgate.com/cgi-bin/article.cgi?f=/c/a/2010/09/20/BUL41FGNJN.DTL
36 http://Wal-Martstores.com/pressroom/news/10514.aspx (accessed May 23, 2011)
37 www.urbanconservancy.org/issues/Wal-Mart
38 www.solidarity-us.org/node/1324
39 http://communitybenefits.blogspot.com/2010/03/nyc-comptroller-lius-cba-task-force.html

7 Wal-Mart at Large

40 www.Wal-Martstores.com/AboutUs/246.aspx (accessed May 21, 2012)
41 http://Wal-Martstores.com/AboutUs/279.aspx (accessed May 29, 2011)
42 http://vimeo.com/12425670
43 "Kalpona Akter, Bangladeshi Sweatshops, and Wal-Mart." Available online at: www.youtube.com/watch?v=oXgdpvhrfQc (accessed May 21, 2012).
44 "Kalpona Akter, Bangladesh Sweatshops, and Wal-Mart" www.youtube.com/watch?v=oXgdpvhrfQc
45 Leslie Dach. "Sustainability Agricultural Remarks" October 14, 2010 http://Walmart stores.com/pressroom/news/10395.aspx
46 Available online at: www.laborrights.org/creating-a-sweatfree-world (accessed June 1, 2011)
47 "Top 10 ways Wal-Mart made a difference in 2011" www.Wal-Martstores.com/sites/responsibility-report/2012/top10.aspx
48 http://thinksocialist.blogspot.com/2006/05/subcomandante-marcos-speaks-out.html
49 Fewer than 7,000 had participated in their Global Direct Farm Program by 2012 www.Wal-Martstores.com/sites/responsibility-report/2012/top10.aspx
50 http://vimeo.com/12425670

8 Wal-Mart and Freedom

51 www.globalcommonsfoundation.org/programme.html
52 Already the free floating "Occupy" label has been appropriated by anti-Wal-Mart activist, Al Norman in his new book *Occupy Wall Mart* (2012)

WORKS CITED

Amnesty International. 2007. "Mexico: The First Anniversary of San Salvador Atenco—Untouchable Impunity?" May 25. Accessed June 18, 2012. www.amnesty.org/en/library/asset/AMR41/018/2007/en/730930de-d396–11dd-a329–2f46302a8cc6/amr41018 2007en.html.

Anderson, Benedict. 1991. *Imagined Communities: Reflections on the Origin and Spread of Nationalism.* London: Verso.

Associated Press. 2009. "$17.5 Million in Wal-Mart Black Truckers' Suit Final." Accessed June 18, 2012. www.thetrucker.com/News/Stories/2009/7/9/175MsettlementinWal-Mart-blacktruckerssuitfinal.aspx.

Backer, Larry Catá. 2007. "Economic Globalization and the Rise of Efficient Systems of Global Private Law Making: Wal-Mart as Global Legislator." *Connecticut Law Review,* (39)4: 1739.

Bajaj, Vikas. 2012. "As Grain Piles Up, India's Poor Still Go Hungry." *The New York Times,* June 7. Accessed June 12, 2012. www.nytimes.com/2012/06/08/business/global/a-failed-food-system-in-india-prompts-an-intense-review.html?_r=1&pagewanted=all.

Barbaro, Michael and Steven Greenhouse. 2006. "Wal-Mart Image-Builder Resigns." *The New York Times,* August 18.

Barstow, David. 2012. "Vast Mexico Bribery Case Hushed Up by Wal-Mart after Top-Level Struggle." *The New York Times,* April 21.

Basker, Emek. 2005. "Job Creation or Destruction? Labor Market Effects of Wal-Mart Expansion." *Review of Economics and Statistics,* 87(1): 174–183.

Basker, Emek. 2007. "The Causes and Consequences of Wal-Mart's Growth." *The Journal of Economic Perspectives,* 21(3): 177–198.

Bello, Walden. 2008. "Manufacturing a Food Crisis." *The Nation,* May 15.

Benson, Peter and Stuart Kirsh. 2010. "Capitalism and the Politics of Resignation." *Current Anthropology,* 51(4): 459–486.

Berlant, Lauren. 1997. *The Queen of America Goes to Washington City: Essays on Sex and Citizenship.* Durham, NC: Duke University Press.

Berlant, Lauren. 2011. *Cruel Optimism.* Durham, NC: Duke University Press.

Bianco, Anthony. 2006. *The Bully of Bentonville: How the High Cost of Wal-Mart's Everyday Prices is Hurting America.* New York: Currency/Doubleday Press.

Bielby, William. 2005. "Applying Social Research on Stereotyping and Cognitive Bias to Employment Discrimination Litigation: The Case of Allegations of Systematic Gender Bias. In *Handbook of Employment Discrimination Research,* Laura Beth Nielson and Robert Nelson (Eds.), 395–408. New York: Springer.

Blanchard, Cherie, Comm, Clare L., and Dennis F.X. Mathaisel. 2008. "Adding Value to Service Providers: Benchmarking at Wal-Mart." *Benchmarking: An International Journal,* 15(2): 166–177.

Brown, Wendy. 1995. *States of Injury: Power and Freedom in Late Capitalism*. Princeton, NJ: Princeton University Press.

Chan, Anita. 2011. *Wal-Mart in China*. Ithaca, NY: Cornell University Press.

Chan, Anita and Jonathan Unger. 2011. "Wal-Mart's China Connections." *The American Prospect*, 21(4): A15–A17.

Chavez, Manuel. 2002. "The Transformation of Mexican Retailing with NAFTA." *Development Policy Review*, 20(4): 503–513.

Cho, Eunice Hyunhe, Anastasia Christman, Maurice Emsellem, Catherine K. Ruckelshaus, and Rebecca Smith. 2011. "Chain of Greed: How Wal-Mart's Domestic Outsourcing Produces Everyday Low Wages and Poor Working Conditions for Warehouse Workers." Accessed June 6, 2012. National Employment Law Project, June. www.nelp.org/page/-/Justice/2012/ChainOfGreed.pdf?nocdn=1.

Clifford, Stephanie and Steven Greenhouse. 2012. "Wal-Mart's U.S. Expansion Plans Complicated by Bribery Scandal." *The New York Times*, April 30.

Collins, Jane. May 26, 2006. "The Opposite of Fordism: Wal-Mart Rolls Back a Regime of Accumulation." Paper presented at the "What's Wrong With America?" conference. Accessed June 6, 2012. www.dces.wisc.edu/documents/faculty-books/collins/Collins-Wal-Mart.pdf.

Copeland, Nicholas. 2011. "'Guatemala Will Never Change': Radical Pessimism and the Politics of Personal Interest in the Guatemalan Highlands." *Journal of Latin American Studies*, (43)3: 485–515.

Crenshaw, Kimberlé. 1991. "Mapping the Margins: Intersectionality, Identity Politics, and Violence against Women of Color." *Stanford Law Review*, 43(6): 1241–1299.

Davis, Julie, David Merriman, Lucia Samoya, Brian Flanagan, Ron Baiman, and Joe Persky. 2009. "The Impact of an Urban Wal-Mart Store on Area Businesses: An Evaluation of One Chicago Neighborhood's Experience." Chicago, IL: Center for Urban Research and Learning, Loyola University. Accessed June 2, 2012. www.luc.edu/curl/pdfs/Media/Wal-MartReport21010_01_11.pdf.

Davis, Mike. 2006. *Planet of Slums*. London: Verso.

Denniston, Lyle. 2011. "Argument Preview: Wal-Mart and Worker's Rights." *SCOTUSblog*, March 28. www.scotusblog.com/?p=116759.

Denyer, Simon. 2011. "India Turns to Wal-Mart as Food Prices Rise." *The Washington Post*, February 25.

Dicker, John. 2005. *The United States of Wal-Mart*. New York: Penguin.

Drucker, Peter. 1972. *Concept of the Corporation*. 2nd ed. New York: John Day Company.

Dube, Arindrajit and Ken Jacobs. 2004a. "Hidden Cost of Wal-Mart Jobs: Use of Safety Net Programs by Wal-Mart Workers in California." Berkeley, CA: UC Berkeley Centre for Labor Research and Education. Accessed June 6, 2012. http://laborcenter.berkeley.edu/retail/Wal-Mart.pdf.

Dube, Arindrajit and Ken Jacobs. 2004b. "Wal-Mart's New Health Care Plan: Medicaid." Accessed June 7, 2012. http://WalMartwatch.com/wpcontent/blogs.dir/2/files/pdf/medicaid_factsheet.pdf.

Dube, Arindrajit, T. William Lester, and Barry Eidlin. 2007. "A Downward Push: The Impact of Wal-Mart Stores on Retail Wage and Benefits." Berkeley: CA: UC Berkeley Center for Labor Research and Education. Accessed June 18, 2012. http://laborcenter.berkeley.edu/retail/walmart_downward_push07.pdf.

Duggan, Lisa. 2003. *The Twilight of Equality: Neoliberalism, Cultural Politics, and the Attack on Democracy*. New York: Beacon Press.

Dukes v. Wal-Mart Inc., 509 F. 3d 1168 – Court of Appeals, 9th Circuit 2007. Accessed June 11, 2011. www.supremecourt.gov/opinions/10pdf/10-277.pdf.

Durand, Cédric. 2007. "Externalities from Foreign Direct Investment in the Mexican Retailing Sector." *Cambridge Journal of Economics*, 31: 393–411.

Ehrenreich, Barbara. 2011a. "Wal-Mart—It's Alive!" *American Prospect*, March 29.

Ehrenreich, Barbara. 2011*b*. *Nickled and Dimed: On (Not) Getting By in America*. New York: Picador.

Escobar, Arturo. (1995) *Encountering Development: The Making and Unmaking of the Third World*. Princeton, NJ: Princeton University Press.

Farmer, Paul. 2004. *Pathologies of Power: Health, Human Rights, and the New War on the Poor*. Berkeley, CA: University of California Press.

Featherstone, Liza. 2005*a*. *Selling Women Short: The Landmark Battle for Workers' Rights at Wal-Mart*. New York: Basic.

Featherstone, Liza. 2005*b*. "Down and Out in Discount America." *The Nation*, January 3.

Featherstone, Liza. 2011. "Fighting Back." *The American Prospect*, 21(4): A20–A22.

Fishman, Charles. 2005. *The Wal-Mart Effect: How the World's Most Powerful Company Really Works—and How It's Transforming the American Economy*. New York: Penguin.

"Fling Wide the Gates: India Should Throw off its Caution about Opening Up to Foreign Investment." 2011. *The Economist*, April 4. Accessed November 20, 2012. http://www.economist.com/node/18560557.

Foucault, Michel. 1979. *Discipline and Punish: The Birth of the Prison*. New York: Vintage.

Frank, Thomas. 2004. *What's the Matter with Kansas? How Conservatives Won the Heart of America*. New York: Henry Holt.

Garrett, Allison. 2008. "The Corporation as Sovereign." *Maine Law Review*, (60)1: 129–164.

Gieryn, Thomas F. 2000. "A Space for Place in Sociology." *Annual Review of Sociology*, 26: 463–496.

Goswami, Rahul. 2012. "Food and Agriculture: Trends in India into the Early Twelfth Plan Period." *Macroscan*, April 23. Accessed October 2, 2012. http://macroscan.com/pol/apr12/pol230412Food_Agri.htm.

Graff, Thomas O. 2006. "Unequal Competition among Chains of Supercenters: Kmart, Target, and Wal-Mart." *The Professional Geographer*, 58(1): 54–64.

Greenhouse, Steven. 2005. "Fired Officer is Suing Wal-Mart." *The New York Times*, July 1.

Greenhouse, Steven. 2011. "Wal-Mart Workers Try the Non-union Route." *The New York Times*, June 14.

Hardt, Michael and Antonio Negri. 2000. *Empire*. Cambridge, MA: Harvard University Press.

Harvey, David. 1989. *The Condition of Postmodernity: An Enquiry into the Origins of Cultural Change*. Cambridge, MA: Blackwell Press.

Harvey, David. 2007. *A Brief History of Neoliberalism*. Oxford: Oxford University Press.

Hays, Constance L. 2004. "What Wal-Mart Knows About Its Customers." *The New York Times*, November 14.

Herman, Charlie. 2010. "New York City Council Postpones Wal-Mart Hearing." *WNYC News*, December 10. Accessed June 1, 2011. www.wnyc.org/articles/wnyc-news/2010/dec/10/new-york-city-council-postpones-wal-mart-hearing/.

Hilton, Matthew. 2000. "Class, Consumption and the Public Sphere." *Journal of Contemporary History*, 35(4): 655–666.

Ho, Karen. 2009. *Liquidated: An Ethnography of Wall Street*. Durham, NC: Duke University Press.

Human Rights Watch. 1999. "The Price of Oil: Corporate Social Responsibility and Human Rights Violations in Nigeria's Oil Producing Communities." Accessed June 18, 2012. www.hrw.org/reports/1999/nigeria/nigeria0199.pdf.

Human Rights Watch. 2007. "Discounting Rights: Wal-Mart's Violation of U.S. Workers' Right to Freedom of Association." Accessed June 18, 2012. www.hrw.org/reports/2007/04/30/discounting-rights.

Humes, Edward. 2011. *Force of Nature: The Unlikely Story of Wal-Mart's Green Revolution*. New York: Harper Collins.

Iacovone, Leonardo, Beata Javorcik, Wolfgang Keller, and James Tybout. 2011. "Supplier Responses to Wal-Mart's Invasion of Mexico." Last accessed June 18, 2012. www.econ.yale.edu/seminars/IntTrade/it12/Tybout-120418.pdf.

International Labor Rights Forum. 2007. "Ethical Standards and Working Conditions in Wal-Mart's Supply Chain." Accessed June 1, 2012. hwww.laborrights.org/creating-a-sweatfree-world/wal-mart-campaign.

Jacobs, Ken, Dave Graham-Shire, and Stephanie Luce. April 2011. "Living Wage Policies and Big-Box Retail: How a Higher Wage Standard Would Impact Shoppers." Berkeley, CA: UC Berkeley Center for Labor Research and Education. Accessed June 1, 2012. http://laborcenter.berkeley.edu/research/Wal-Mart.shtml.

Javorcik, B., W. Keller, and J. Tybout. 2008. "Openness and Industrial Responses in a Wal-Mart World: A Case Study of Mexican Soaps, Detergents and Surfactant Producers." *World Economy*: 1558–1580. December.

Jia, Panle. 2007. "What Happens When Wal-Mart Comes To Town: An Empirical Analysis of the Discount Industry." Accessed October 2, 2012. http://economics.mit.edu/files/7575.

Jones, Sandra. 2010. "Dress for Success Scouts Space in Chicago for Regional Office." *The Chicago Tribune*, August 2. Accessed June 20, 2011. http://articles.chicagotribune.com/2010–08–02/business/ct-biz-0802-dress-for-success-20100802_1_interview-suit-wal-mart-stores-dress.

Jones, Van. 2012. "The 99 Percent for the 100 Percent: The Case for Deep Patriotism." *The Nation*, April 2. Accessed June 1, 2012. www.thenation.com/article/167172/99-%100-%-case-deep-patriotism

Juhasz, Antonia. 2005. "What Wal-Mart Wants from NAFTA." *Alternet*, December 13. Accessed June 10, 2012. www.alternet.org/economy/29464?page=2.

Karjanen, David. 2006. "The Wal-Mart Effect and the New Face of Capitalism: Labor Market and Community Impacts of the Mega Retailer." In *Wal-Mart: The Face of Twenty-First Century Capitalism*, Nelson Lichtenstein (Ed.), 143–162. New York: The New Press.

Kipple, Adam, Andrew Kipple, and Luke Wherry. 2010. *People of Wal-Mart.com: Shop & Awe*. Naperville, IL: Sourcebooks.

Knorr, Andreas and Andreas Arndt. 2003. "Why Did Wal-Mart Fail in Germany?" Accessed June 1, 2012. www.iwim.uni-bremen.de/publikationen/pdf/w024.pdf.

Larsen, Kristian and Jason Gilliland. 2009. "A Farmer's Market in a Food Desert: Evaluating Impacts on the Price and Availability of Healthy Food." *Health and Place*, 15(4): 1158–2116.

Lester, T. William and Ken Jacobs. 2010. "Creating Good Jobs in Our Communities: How Higher Wage Standards Affect Economic Development and Employment." Washington, DC: Center for American Progress Action Fund (American WorkerProject). Accessed June 1, 2012. www.americanprogressaction.org/issues/2010/11/pdf/living_wage.pdf.

Lichtenstein, Nelson. 2009. *The Retail Revolution: How Wal-Mart Created a Brave New World of Business*. New York: Picador.

Lichtenstein, Nelson. 2011*a*. "Wal-Mart Tries to Go to Town." *The American Prospect*, 21(4): A7–A11.

Lichtenstein, Nelson. 2011*b*. "Wal-Mart's Authoritarian Culture." *The New York Times*, June 21.

Lydersen, Kari. 2011. "Stolen Wages and Death Sentences: Stories from the Wal-Mart Worker Tour." *In These Times*, March 29.

Lynn, Barry. July 2006. "Breaking the Chain." *Harper's*. Accessed June 1, 2012. www.harpers.org/archive/2006/07/0081115.

Lynn, Barry and Philip Longman. May 4, 2010. "Who Broke America's Job Machine." *Washington Monthly*. Accessed June 1, 2012. www.washingtonmonthly.com/features/2010/1003.lynn-longman.html.

Maestri, Nicole. 2008. "Wal-Mart.com CEO Says Sales Grow Despite Downturn." *Reuters*, November 13. Accessed June 18, 2012. www.reuters.com/article/2008/11/13/us-Wal-Mart-website-interview-idUSTRE4AC92720081113.

Marcos, Subcomandante. 2001. "The Fourth World War." *La Jornada*, October 23.

Meeks, Margot and Rachel J.C. Chen. 2011. "Can Walmart Integrate Values with Value? From Sustainability to Sustainable Business." *Journal of Sustainable Development*, 4(5): 62–66.

Meyer, Stephen. 1981. *The Five Dollar Day: Labor Management and Social Control in the Ford Motor Company, 1908–1921.* Albany, NY: SUNY Press.

Meyerson, Harold. 2005. "Open Doors, Closed Minds: How One Wal-Mart True Believer Was Ex-communicated for His Faith in Doing What He Thought the Company Expected of Him: Crying Foul." *The American Prospect,* 16(12): 32–34.

Meyerson, Harold. 2011. "Which Path for Europe?" *The American Prospect.* May, A18–A19.

Miles, Kathleen. 2012. "Wal-Mart in LA: Chinatown Store Protestors Say Wal-Mart Employees Rely on Welfare." *The Huffington Post,* March 9. Accessed June 1, 2012. www.huffington post.com/2012/03/09/Wal-Mart-la-chinatown-protesters_n_1333392.html.

Mitchell, Stacy. 2012. "Wal-Mart's Greenwash: Why the Retail Giant is Still Unsustainable." *Grist,* November 7. http://grist.org/series/2011–11–07-Wal-Mart-greenwash-retail-giant-still-unsustainable/.

Moberg, David. 2011. "How Wal-Mart Shapes the World." *The American Prospect,* May 2011: A3–A6.

Moreton, Bethany. 2009. *To Serve God and Wal-Mart: The Making of Christian Free Enterprise.* Cambridge, MA: Harvard University Press.

Mui, Ylan. 2011. "Wal-Mart Works with Unions Abroad, But Not at Home." *The Washington Post,* June 7. Accessed June 10, 2012. www.washingtonpost.com/business/economy/wal-mart-works-with-unions-abroad-but-not-at-home/2011/06/07/AG0nOPLH_story.html.

Neff, Jack. 2008. "Wal-Mart Aggressively Courts Mommy Bloggers" *Advertising Age,* November 24. Accessed June 6, 2011. www.commercialalert.org/news/archive/2008/11/wal-mart-aggressively-courts-mommy-bloggers.

Neumark, David, Junfu Zhang, and Stephen Ciccarella. 2008. "The Effects of Wal-Mart on Local Labor Markets." *Journal of Urban Economics,* 63(2): 405–430.

Norman, Al. 2004. *The Case Against Wal-Mart.* New York: Raphael Marketing.

Northrup, Laura. 2011. "The World's Smallest Wal-Mart Opens on a College Campus." *The Consumerist,* January 20. http://consumerist.com/2011/01/the-worlds-smallest-Wal-Mart-opens-on-a-college-campus.html.

Pot, Anna, John Howchin, and Kris Douma. 2011. "Good Labour Relations Aid Retailers' Success." *Financial Times,* June 19. Accessed June 10, 2012. www.ft.com/intl/cms/s/0/384bbbfe-95bd-11e0-8f82-00144feab49a.html#axzz1iW4gOBa2.

Quinn, Bill. 2005. *How Wal-Mart is Destroying America (and the World), and What You Can Do About It.* Berkeley, CA: Ten Speed Press.

Reich, R. 2010. *Aftershock: The Next Economy and America's Future.* New York: Vintage Books.

Rose, Nikolas. 1996. "Governing 'Advanced' Liberal Democracies." In *Foucault and Political Reason: Liberalism, Neoliberalism and Rationalities of Government,* A. Barry, T. Osborne and N. Rose (Eds.), 37–64. Chicago, IL: University of Chicago Press.

Rose, Nikolas. 1999. *Powers of Freedom: Reframing Political Thought.* Cambridge: Cambridge University Press.

Ross, John. 2005. "Wal-Mart Invades Mexico." *Counterpunch,* March 17. Accessed June 18, 2012. www.counterpunch.org/2005/03/17/wal-mart-invades-mexico/.

Ross, John. 2008. "Agrarian Apocalypse Looms in Mexico." *ZMagazine,* March. Accessed June 1, 2012. www.zcommunications.org/agrarian-apocolypse-looms-in-mexico-by-john-ross.

Rowe, Jonathan. 2011. "The Greening of Wal-Mart." *The American Prospect,* April 19. Accessed October 2, 2012. http://prospect.org/article/greening-wal-mart.

Rushe, Dominic. 2011. "Wal-Mart Sex-Bias Case Divides US Supreme Court." *The Guardian,* March 30. Accessed June 1, 2011. www.guardian.co.uk/law/2011/mar/28/Wal-Mart-sex-discrimination-case-supreme-court.

Sacks, Danielle. 2007. "Working With the Enemy." *Fast Company,* September 1. Accessed November 20, 2012. http://www.fastcompany.com/60374/working-enemy.

Salkin, Patricia and Amy Lavine. 2008. "Understanding Community Benefits Agreements: Equitable Development, Social Justice and Other Considerations for Developers,

Municipalities and Community Organizations." *UCLA Journal of Environmental Law & Policy*, 26. Albany Law School Research Paper No. 09–04.

Sainath, P. 2010. "Centre has no Money for Universal PDS." *The Hindu*, September 18.

Sainath. P. 2011. "FDI in Retail—UPA 'Retired Hurt.'" *The Hindu*, December 12. Accessed June 10, 2012. www.thehindu.com/opinion/lead/article2706988.ece.

Schmitt, John and David Rosnick. 2011. "The Wage and Employment Impact of Minimum-Wage Laws in Three Cities." Washington DC: Center for Economic Policy and Research. Accessed June 18, 2012. www.cepr.net/documents/publications/min-wage-2011-03.pdf.

Schwentesius, R. and Gomez, M.A. 2002. "The Rise of Supermarkets in Mexico: Impact on Horticulture Chains." *Development Policy Review*, 20(4): 487–502.

Sen, Amartya. 2001. *Development as Freedom*. New York: Knopf.

Serwer, Andy. 2005. "Bruised in Bentonville." *FORTUNE Magazine*, April 18. Accessed June 1, 2012. http://money.cnn.com/magazines/fortune/fortune_archive/2005/04/18/8257005/index.htm.

Shapiro, Lila. 2012. "Wal-Mart Blacklisted By Major Pension Fund Over Poor Labor Practices." *The Huffington Post*, January 5. Accessed June 10, 2012. www.huffingtonpost.com/2012/01/05/Wal-Mart-blacklist-abp-pension-fund_n_1186384.html.

Shiva, Vandana. 2006. "Interview with Amy Goodman." *Democracy Now*, December 13. Accessed June 6, 2012. www.democracynow.org/2006/12/13/vandana_shiva_on_farmer_suicides_the.

Shiva, Vandana. 2007. "How to Address Humanity's Global Crisis?" *Environmental News Network*. October 2. Accessed June 6, 2012. www.enn.com/lifestyle/article/23551/print.

Stewart, Kathleen. 2007. *Ordinary Affects*. Durham, NC: Duke University Press.

Stiglitz, Joseph. 2002. *Globalization and its Discontents*. New York: Norton.

Stiglitz, Joseph. 2012. *The Price of Inequality: How Today's Divided Society Endangers Our Future*. New York: Norton.

Stiglitz, Joseph and Andrew Charlton. 2005. *Fair Trade for All*. Oxford: Oxford University Press.

Stone, Kenneth. 1995. "Impact of Wal-Mart Stores and Other Mass Merchandisers in Iowa, 1983–1993." *Iowa State University, Economic Development Review*, Spring: 60–70.

Stone, Kenneth, Georganne Artz, and Albert Myles. 2002. "The Economic Impact of Wal-Mart Supercenters on Existing Businesses in Mississippi." Mississippi State, MS: Mississippi State University Extension Service.

Strasser, Susan. 2006. "Woolworth to Wal-Mart: Mass Merchandising and the Changing Culture of Consumption." In *Wal-Mart: The Face of Twenty-First Century Capitalism*, Nelson Lichtenstein (Ed.), 31–56. New York: The New Press.

Subcommandante Marcos. 2001. "The Fourth World War." *NarcoNews*, November 9. Accessed June 18, 2012. www.narconews.com/zmarcosfourthworldwar.html.

Swamy, Shekhar. 2012. "A Mexican Warning on Retail FDI." *The Hindu Business Line*, May 29. Accessed June 12, 2012. www.thehindubusinessline.com/opinion/article3469898.ece.

Thomas, Chris. 2006. "Massacre in Atenco: Violence, Politics and Other Campaigns in Mexico." Colectivos de Apoyo, Solidaridad y Acción. Issue 36, May. Accessed June 6, 2012. www.casacollective.org/en/story/analysis/massacre-atenco-violence-politics-and-other-campaigns-mexico.

Tilly, Chris. 2006. "Wal-Mart in Mexico: The Limits of Growth." In *Wal-Mart: The Face of Twenty-First Century Capitalism*, Nelson Lichtenstein (Ed.), 201–209. New York: The New Press.

United Food and Commercial Workers. 2010. "Ending Wal-Mart's Rural Stranglehold." Accessed June 1, 2012. www.ufcw.org/docUploads/AG %20Consolidation %20White %20Paper2.pdf?CFID=13930665&CFTOKEN=33799203.

Walker, Margath, David Walker, and Yanga Villagómez Velásquez. 2006. "The Wal-Martification of Teotihuacan: Issues of Resistance and Cultural Heritage." In *Wal-Mart World: The*

World's Biggest Corporation in the Global Economy, Stanley D. Brunn (Ed.), 213–224. New York: Routledge.

Wallerstein, Immanuel. 2004. *World Systems Analysis: An Introduction*. Durham, NC: Duke University Press.

Wal-Mart. 1997. "Wal-Mart: A Manager's Toolbox to Remaining Union Free." Accessed June 18, 2012. www.reclaimdemocracy.org/Wal-Mart/antiunionman.pdf.

Wal-Mart Stores. 2011. "The Wal-Mart Foundation Donates $2 Million to Help Unemployed Women Get Back to Work." Accessed June 18, 2012. http://nyc.Wal-Martcommunity. com/the-Wal-Mart-foundation-donates-2-million-to-help-unemployed-women-get-back-to-work/.

Wal-Mart Watch. 2008. "Wal-Mart's New Health Plan: Medicaid." Accessed June 21, 2012. http://walmartwatch.com/wp-content/blogs.dir/2/files/pdf/medicaid_factsheet.pdf.

Walton, Sam. 1992. "Sam's Rules for Building a Business." Bentonville, AR: Wal-Mart Stores.

Walton, Sam and John Huey. 1993. *Made In America*. New York: Bantam.

Whitacre, Paula Tarnapol, Peggy Tsai, and Janet Mulligan (National Research Council). 2009. "The Public Health Effects of Food Deserts: Workshop Summary." Washington, DC: National Academies Press. Accessed October 2, 2012. www.nap.edu/catalog.php ?record_id=12623.

Whitaker, Jan. 2006. *Service and Style: How the American Department Store Fashioned the Middle Class*. New York: St. Martin's Press.

Winne, Mark. 2008. *Closing the Food Gap: Resetting the Table in the Land of Plenty*. New York: Beacon Press.

Wolf, Eric. 1982. *Europe and the People without History*. Berkeley, CA: University of California Press.

Woodman, Spencer. 2012. "Labor Takes Aim at Wal-Mart—Again." *The Nation*, January 23. Accessed June 1, 2012. www.thenation.com/article/165437/labor-takes-aim-Wal-Mart-again.

INDEX

References to illustrations/photographs will be in *italics*.

THE SOCIAL ISSUES
COLLECTION™

Finally, it's easy to
customize materials for your sociology course

Choose from a collection of 250 readings from Routledge and other publishers to create a perfect anthology that fits your course and students.

1 Go to the website at
socialissuescollection.com

2 Choose from 250
readings in sociology

3 Create your complete
custom anthology

Readings from The Social Issues Collection are pre-cleared and available at reduced permission rates, helping your students save money on course materials. Projects are ready in 2 weeks for direct e-commerce student purchases.

For over 25 undergraduate sociology courses including:

Criminology	Globalization	Social Inequalities
Cultural Sociology	Sociology of Work and Economy	Sociology of Media and Communication
Environmental Sociology	Marriage and Family	Sociology of Place
Gender	Race and Ethnicity	Sociology of Religion